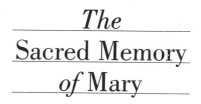

The
Sacred Memory
of Mary

The
Sacred Memory
of Mary

Walter T. Brennan, O.S.M.

PAULIST PRESS/ NEW YORK/ MAHWAH

Text design by Ellen Whitney

Library of Congress Cataloging-in-Publication Data

Brennan, Walter T., 1935-
    The sacred memory of Mary/Walter T. Brennan.
      p. cm.
    Includes bibliographies.
    ISBN 0-8091-2955-8 (pbk.)
    1. Mary, Blessed Virgin, Saint—Theology—History. 2. Bible.
N.T. Gospels—Criticism, interpretation, etc. 3. Mary, Blessed
Virgin, Saint—Cult—History. I. Title.
BT611.B73 1988
232.91—dc19   87-28761
                                                 CIP

Published by Paulist Press
997 Macarthur Boulevard
Mahwah, NJ 07430

Printed and bound in the
United States of America

CONTENTS

"Remember, because you have been saved from darkness and have been brought into God's kingdom and light."

Pope St. Leo the Great

1

TO REFRESH OUR MEMORIES

> Joined to Christ the Head, and in communion with all his saints, the faithful must in the first place reverence the memory "of the glorious ever Virgin Mary, Mother of God and of our Lord Jesus Christ." . . . She is hailed as pre-eminent and as a wholly unique member of the Church, and as its type and outstanding model in faith and charity.[1]

Those strong words were the message of the Second Vatican Council to the whole Church. They were proclaimed in 1964. That was over twenty years ago.

Notice those words "reverence the memory" of Mary. The Council chose those words carefully. Memory is the key to understanding Mary. It is through memory that we know about anyone from the past. But it is through a special kind of memory that the Church says we can not only know about Mary, but we can know and reverence her.

It is important to examine this special kind of memory. Only then will we be able to do what the Council said we "must" do. And we have not really done so. The early Church remembered her and knew her with reverence. That memory and knowledge went on for almost twenty centuries. But now it is at a low point. It seems as if a kind of senility has crept into the Church. For many Catholics Mary has "been placed on the edge of life and devotion simply because she is not known," as one recent study put it.[2]

To examine this special kind of memory of Mary in the Church we can begin with some reflection upon the connection between *memory* and *knowledge*. With that connection as our starting point we may learn more about the memory of Mary which we "must" reverence "in the first place."

All of us know, if we think about it, that we have to *know about* someone before we can *know* that person. That is the way we meet people in daily life. We *know about* them before we get to *know* them. Someone we get to know is someone we have encountered at first in a superficial way. There has to be some kind of physical meeting at first. It may not even be an introduction. Perhaps we see someone and like his or her appearance. This spurs us on to know more about the person. Or we might have a chance encounter. We might "meet someone by accident" in a supermarket. We see someone who is wearing a T-shirt or hat from our home town, and we strike up "small talk." The next step is to learn the other person's name. Then, if there is enough reason for it, we meet again. Eventually we spend more time together. Slowly we get to "know someone better." Still we do not really "know" a person unless we care to spend time with him or her. Because we care, we may even learn about the other person's intimate life. If there is care and trust there is eventually a mutual opening of self to self. However that happens, only then can we say that we "know" each other. We have moved from "knowing about" someone to "knowing" that person.

What is interesting about the way we know about someone or come to know that person in a more intimate way is that memory has a distinct role to play in the processes. Memory is the key to the continuity of our knowledge. We will never *know about* things or people unless we remember the details of what or who they are from the start. By memory we recognize that it is the same things or persons we see as we continue to gain knowledge about them. We know that "this is the way I turned on the machine before," or that "this is the person I met before at the supermarket." And as our knowledge about someone grows into personal knowledge of that person, memory becomes even more. It is the key to unity. In more intimate knowledge our own memory becomes involved with the other person's memory. We remember together the moments we shared and what they meant. In the absence of the other person my memory allows me to be present to him or her. I remember and imagine and know "you" despite "your" distance from me when you are my friend.

Memory and knowledge are linked together. Memory is the key to continuity and unity in knowing about someone and in getting to really know him or her.

The relationship between memory and knowledge has even more to it. Memory is also the key by which we can get to know about, or even in some way know, a person from the past.

This further role of memory is obvious in history. We can *know about* persons and events of the past. As we encounter records—be they written accounts or monuments—we begin to piece together a story of someone long gone. With a critical eye we can ascertain details that increase our knowledge about someone. There is a great thrill in moving from a pyramid tomb to translated hieroglyphics and getting to know about King Tut. We gain accurate knowledge about someone if we study history in a scientific way. That is memory aided by critical study of records.

It gets even more interesting to note that the more personal the records are of someone from the past—say an autobiography or letters written to a friend—we feel we are "getting to know" someone from the past in a more personal way. Somehow, through our memory, we can imagine how this person thought or acted. For example, I can *know about* St. Augustine of Hippo. I can grow to know many details about him and the way he thought from studying critical editions of his theological works. But when I share his thoughts and memories which he recorded in a very personal way in his *Confessions* I begin to feel I *know* him more intimately. Of course to do this I have to depend on the critical history which lets me first *know about* Saint Augustine and which ensures that I am truly sharing what were his own thoughts when I read the *Confessions*. Critical history saves me from the error of attributing to St. Augustine what he did not actually write. It also saves me from reading into the *Confessions* my own thoughts about what he might have said if he were I.

Now all of this, and something more, as we shall see, applies to our memory and knowledge of Mary. There are records about Mary—the Gospels. These allow us to *know about* her. If we use critical historical methods of study, to avoid the errors of attributing to her what the Gospels do not attribute to her or of reading my own thoughts into the Gospels instead of reading out of them what they really say about Mary, we can be sure that what we know about her is accurate. And we can go further, reading the Gospels, especially the words attributed to her as prayers, with the same spirit of prayer. This assures me that I am sharing the same kind of prayer which the Church put upon her lips in the Gospels. I begin to feel that I *know* her more intimately.

But there is something more involved in the memory of Mary. This "something more" was already implied above when we mentioned "the Church" and "prayer." It means this. Critical historical study of the Gospels leads us to the Church and its memory of Mary, not to a biography or autobiography of her. Then we can *know about* Mary as the Church remembered her within the story of Jesus. To go further, to be able to use our memory not only for continuity in our knowledge but for unity with the Mary we know about from the Church's memory, we will have to be able to have the same spirit of faith and prayer which the Church's intimate memory of her contains.

When we use our memories to study the life and works of St. Augustine we get to *know about* Augustine as historians. We have to use critical historical methods to establish which texts are ones he actually wrote, and literary methods to sort out what form of writing he used to convey various kinds of ideas, such as dialogues or sermons or meditations. We have to know that our translation is accurate. We have to know the social milieu in which he wrote to understand his references to certain ideas and events. And we have to know quite a lot about philosophy and theology and the Bible in order to interpret his ideas intelligently. Then we can move from the Augustine we *know about* to the Augustine of the *Confessions* whom we can get *to know* personally, granted that this personal knowledge is limited by many factors.

With Mary we have to do that, but more. We must use historical and other studies to reach the point of *knowing about* Mary from the Gospels. But it will be impossible to have even the limited *personal knowledge* of her that we could have of an Augustine unless we enter the whole story of the Gospels of which her story is a part. In the case of St. Augustine we can come to *know about* him directly, from his own works, and then move on—perhaps—to a personal empathy with him. In the case of Mary we cannot get to *know about* her directly. We can only get to *know about* the Mary whom the Church portrayed in her prayer and faith as part of the story of

Jesus the Lord. We have no biography or autobiography of her, and no writings by her. We have no ideas of her own, nor words, that can be separated from the Church's religious faith as presented in the unique literary forms we call Gospels. The way the Church remembered Mary, as part of the proclamation of the good news of Jesus, and the way the Church composed the Gospels by using literary figures to express her religious faith in terms of the Hebrew Scriptures, is what we can *know about*. But if we share the faith and the religious outlook of the Church, if we pray the Magnificat prayer of Mary in the Gospel of Luke with the faith and sense of fulfillment of the Hebrew Scriptures in that Gospel, then we can begin to get *to know* Mary.

In other words, we can come to know Mary through memory. But that will demand more than even the most accurate historical knowledge. It will demand faith—the kind of faith which is in the Gospels, the kind of faith which is the memory of Jesus as Lord. Our memories will have to be one with the memory of the Church which gave us the Gospels.

How powerful memory is, then! Memory, which is the way we get to know about anything or anyone; memory, which is the way we can come to know a person in depth; memory, which is the key to the continuity and to the unity of the knowledge we share with our closest of friends. This memory of ours is the way to get to know Mary.

To get to know Mary again through our memory will demand much of us, however. It will demand study of the Gospels and the Church's sacred memory of the Lord throughout the centuries. There can be no room here for piety which rejects study, just as there can be no room for study without piety. Authentic memory of Mary in the Church will have to be kept free of anything which distorts it, such as pious legends, credulous tales, superstitions which exaggerate her place in God's plan, and naive misunderstandings of the meaning of the Gospels. The Church's memory of Mary will have to be lived and treasured in such a way that it is not reduced to the logical concepts and propositions of a dry theology divorced from the life and liturgy of the whole people of God. It will always have to be part of the proclamation of the story of Jesus, the Lord who revealed in his flesh the loving plan of God for all people.[3]

To meet these demands will not be easy. Ordinary people tend to love visions and extraordinary phenomena more than they do the practice of the Sermon on the Mount. Ethnic groups would rather emphasize their national festive devotions than the common liturgy of the Church. We all would like to have our Gospels say what we would like to hear or have heard before without a great deal of study. Most of us tend to picture religion as asking God for what we need now rather than praise of God's glory and goodness. And all of us have a recent past of fundamentalist reading of Scripture and a rationalistic kind of theology to overcome. The memory of Mary has been covered over with layers of inauthentic images. It won't be easy to get underneath them all to the authentic memory carried on in the Church for centuries.[4]

The Church has called us to a new and fresh approach to the memory of Mary. It has urged us to use the best intellectual tools available to know about Mary. It has asked us to come to know and reverence Mary in the liturgy and in devotions that have been freed from inauthentic images. The Second Vatican Council spelled out what had been a growing concern in the Church for many years beforehand. Bishops and leaders all over the world had become increasingly aware that the authentic memories of the Gospel were being lost. And that included the memory of Mary which had become covered over by non-Gospel devotional images and a very abstract theology of Mary's privileges as Mother of God, Queen of the Universe, the Immaculate Conception, Assumed into Heaven, and Co-Redeemer of the human race. There was little room for the Gospel stories of Jesus and the love of God. The people in general were more interested in apparitions of Mary and miraculous cures than in the practice of the Gospel. The people were hungry for Christ and salvation and were turning to inauthentic images to satisfy their hunger. They wanted and needed the Church's sacred memory of the Lord. And this is what the Pope and bishops and scholars of the Second Vatican Council saw.

The Council outlined the kind of recovery of the tradition that was needed. It was to have as its purpose the return to the Gospels and constant tradition and the removal of what had been cluttering up the memory of the Church. It was to include a renewal of doctrine and liturgy and devotion for the spiritual betterment of all in Church. Its hope was that the Church would incarnate in the present world the mystery of Christ by getting *to know* him better, by becoming more united to him, and by manifesting this sacramental unity with him.

Part of this program for renewal was the recovery of the memory of Mary and the reverence of the Church for her in the first place among all the saints. The Council did what St. Paul told the Romans he did in writing to them: it sought to "refresh our memory" (Rom 15:15).

REFERENCES

1. *The Dogmatic Constitution on the Church*, Vatican II, No. 52, translated by C. O'Neill, O.P., in *Vatican Council II—The Conciliar and Post-Conciliar Documents*, edited by A. Flannery, O.P. (Collegeville: Liturgical Press, 1975), p. 414.

2. *Do Whatever He Tells You—Reflections and Proposals for Promoting Marian Devotion*, 208th General Chapter of the Order of Servants of Mary, with the assistance of the Marianum Pontifical Faculty of Theology. (Rome: General Curia of the Order of Servants of Mary, 1983), p. 47.

3. Pope Paul VI, *Apostolic Exhortation Marialis Cultus*, in *Mary—God's Mother and Ours* (Boston: St. Paul Editions, 1979), Nos. 37, 38, pp. 137, 139.

4. There are two good articles about the relation between emphasis on extraordinary phenomena and poor understanding of doctrine and liturgy in *The Furrow*, 36/10, October 1985: "Apparitions or Christian Witness?" by W. Jeanrond, p. 645, and "The Crisis of the Symbolic Imagination" by Anne F. Kelly, pp. 646–650.

2

FROM "THEN" TO "NOW": THE GROUP MEMORY OF THE CHURCH

J ust as our own individual memory gives us identity as persons—it is the very "belly of our mind," St. Augustine
said—so does a group retain its identity through memory. A group,
like an individual, looks backward to understand the present and
to move forward. By looking to its origins a group remembers where
it came from and where it is going. It remembers "who it is." This
is its "tradition." National groups have their social and civic memories. They celebrate the founding events from which they came.
That is why Americans celebrate the Fourth of July. They remember
the persons and ideals of the Revolutionary War in order to carry
on their tradition of freedom and their identity as heirs of the American Revolution. Other nations do the same. And so do religious
groups.

Every religion is at root a group memory. It is the *sacred memory* of a people which looks back to the group's religious foundation.
It differs from a *secular group memory*, such a national memory that
is civic, because it goes back to creation, absolute beginnings
rather than historical events. Every religion, whether it is a religion
of nature or a religion of revelation from God, is a memory of what
the whole world means from start to finish. All religions are ways of
expressing the meaning of the whole of reality according to how they
see the origin and the final goal of "all creation." Religious people
believe that the world received its meaning "in the beginning," be-

fore time began. Thus Christians believe that the salvation accomplished by Jesus was God's eternal plan from the "beginning."

Religious people live out in their daily lives what they remember is the meaning of the world from its creation. For some it is the endless cycle of fate; for others it is a life of freedom which is a gift of God. In either case the group sacred memory gives meaning to daily life.

Religions celebrate their sacred memory of how life received its meaning from "the beginning" in rituals. In New Year rituals many of the religions of mankind retell and re-enact their story of creation. They remember in word and gesture, as a group, how time was carved out of eternity and given meaning and a goal. At the birth of a baby or at the time of the building of a house or temple or when any important group work is "begun" religious groups re-enact their memory of the sacred beginning of the world and their own group. Memory is handed on and this tradition enables all the members of the religion to live a meaningful life.[1]

This is the human way. Since Christianity is a religion of human beings, it is the Christian way, too. God respects the human nature God created. We believe that God became human in the incarnation of the Word. Jesus revealed his divine Sonship in human ways. Those who believe in this revelation of the divine in and through the human are the religious group called Christians. The Church is a group, the people of God. It is the human group that is the meeting place of the divine and the human, of eternity and time. It is the human group of people who remember that they have received the very life of God through Jesus Christ.

The Church remembers in human ways what life "in Christ" means. The Christian group hands on the sacred memory that all reality comes from God and returns to God our "source and guide and goal" (Rom 11:36). They repeat their story of faith: God the Creator sent the Son to become one of us because of divine love for us, and the Son sent us his Spirit who enables us to pattern our lives on Christ who is the model and purpose of existence. They remember that God "chose us in him before the world began" (Eph 1:4). They celebrate this sacred memory in human rituals: baptism, Eucharist, and their great Passover or feast of the new creation in the passion, death, and resurrection of Jesus. They set down their divine story in human words and literary forms of communication, the Gospels and other writings that became normative for future remembrance in the group. They remember the promise of Jesus that "the Holy Spirit . . . will remind you of all that I told you" (Jn 14:26).

So Christianity is also at root a group memory. Through the sacred group memory of the Church, especially the Scriptures and liturgy, the people of God retain their identity. United in Christ the whole Church remembers where they came from, who they are, and where they are going. As human beings alive with the very life of God, that gift of "sanctifying grace," Christians express their belief and identity through deep symbols of relationship with God. Just as we as individuals need symbols to express our intimate feelings and evaluations, which are part of our knowledge of ourselves and others, so do groups need symbols to express their memory and identity. Religious memory is more than *knowing about* God or life or ourselves. It is *knowledge* of God, of ourselves, and of God's presence among us. Such group memory can never be expressed by mathematical concepts or logical propositions or by "critical objective history" alone. Christians *remember* and *know* through the symbols of their faith.

The memory of Mary in the Church has always been a part of its sacred group memory. In order to recover that memory for our times we will have to use the fresh approach discussed in the previous chapter. It will be important to keep in mind that when we use that approach—study of the Scriptures and of early Church tradition and of liturgy—we will be applying it to "group memory." We will be delving into the stories of our own past as a group, our own traditional memory. We will do this to find our own story today, and Mary's part in it. We will be engaging in a process of recollection that is very deep and very personal for every person in the Church.

Once we understand that our study is that kind of study, it will mean that we will have to have a new approach to the New Testament, especially the Gospels, and to the handing on of the Church's memory in tradition, and to the liturgical expression of our faith. On the one hand we will study history, with the help of all the other academic disciplines that are available, to *know about* our past memories of Mary as a group. On the other hand we will be engaging

in a very personal kind of effort to *know* the Lord of our faith and
Mary's role in our faith. When the early Christians recorded their
memory of Mary as part of their sacred memory of the Lord they
believed that they were meeting Christ in the very present time of
their writing. They were recording and meeting Christ in the full-
ness of his story at the same time. They were witnessing to the ongoing presence of Christ in their group memory of him. Christ, and
his whole mystery, was alive. They *knew* him, and Mary as part of
his present mystery, when they recounted his memory in worship
and in word.

This new approach to the Gospels, to tradition, and to the liturgy will involve us in three kinds of mental effort. The first is what
is technically called *critique*. That means we have to find out to the
best of our abilities what the Gospels or early Church teachers or
the liturgy actually said or say. To do this we have to use critical
historical studies, social studies, studies from comparative religions and from any other field which will enable us to understand
what is being said or communicated in a Gospel or other record. For
example, what is the Gospel of Luke actually saying about Mary in
the infancy stories about Jesus?[2]

Second, we will be involved in what is technically called *hermeneutic*.[3] That means we will have to do our best to discover *what
was meant* by what was said. Now this is a two-sided task. We have
to judge *what was meant* in the past by what was said, and *what that
means today*. It is important to keep in mind that once we find out
that Jesus called God "Abba" or "Father," a tender term, we have
to find out what that meant about God in the Gospels, and we have
to judge what that means today in our Christian faith. It certainly
did not mean then that God was male. Nor does it mean that now.
The early Christian Church had great debates about what Mary's
motherhood of Jesus meant for the Gospels and for their own time.
This involved what Jesus' titles and Jesus' humanity meant in the
Gospels and for their own time. The whole of Christian belief comes
to bear upon the interpretation of each little part of it. No one will
ever be able to judge what was meant by a Christian memory in the
past, or what it might mean now, without entering that world of
Christian belief. To interpret meaning we have to use both reason
and faith.

Third, we will have as our goal what is technically called *an-*

amnesis.[4] This means that we are not merely studying in order to find out what the Gospels said about Mary. Nor are we merely doing that with the added goal of interpreting past statements about Mary in a contemporary way that keeps the same meaning today as in the past. It means that we are going a little deeper, building upon both of those efforts. We are praying, but praying in the sense that we are re-presenting once more, meeting, coming to know and encounter in a personal way, that Mary who is part of the story of Jesus. While this term "anamnesis," like "symbol," has been used mostly in liturgy in order to express the sacramental presence of Christ and his mysteries in our ritual enactments, it also belongs to our entire effort—theological, scriptural, moral, and liturgical—to remember who we are and how we relate to God today. So when we study the words of Mary's Magnificat in Luke's Gospel, we will not only be trying to establish *what* Luke said or *what he meant* by what he said, or *what that means today* for peace and justice. We will be encountering Mary today, praying with her, living our faith.

That all sounds very complex. And it is. We remarked that the study of the memory of Mary would not be easy. But we should not let the technical words throw us off or deter us. If we stop to think about it, every one of us does the same thing every day. We solve our problems by remembering their source, we isolate the factors we have to remedy in a meaningful, present situation, and we move on by integrating our solutions into our personal lives. That is what studying our Church memory of Mary is like. It is very precious and demands a lot of care. Each of us has a personal burden of responsibility to take time and make the effort to relate the "then" of the past to "now" in order to reverence the memory of Mary.

In the following chapters we will reach back to the Church's memory of Mary "then"—in the Scriptures and tradition of the early Church. Our goal will be to understand what the early Church said and meant and prayerfully believed about Mary. Then we will study how the liturgy of the Church developed in order for the Church to know and encounter Christ and Mary's role in his presence in daily life. In other words, we will use *critique* and *hermeneutic* and *anamnesis* to bridge the gap between "then" and "now," past and present. In doing this we will follow the guidelines of the Second Vatican Council: renewal of our memory of Mary as part of our faith in the revelation of Jesus as expressed in the Church's tradition and Scripture and liturgy.

As we undertake those topics it is most important to keep the point of this chapter in mind. The memory of Mary is always the sacred group memory of the Church, in the past and in the present.

Why is that so important to keep in mind? Because the Church's memory of Mary is always our starting point in each of the three kinds of questions we will be asking: What is actually said? What does this mean? How is this meaning a part of my present life?

From the viewpoint of the first question—What do the Scriptures or early tradition and liturgy actually say?—this starting point makes it clear that we are not looking for a history of Mary. Critical studies have enabled us to know that clearly today. The biblical memory of Mary is not a biography of Mary nor a documentary film nor another kind of contemporary history. The temptation to find contemporary kinds of historical thought or writing has to be avoided just as the temptation of a preacher to find on every page of the Bible what he or she wants should be shunned. The Bible, and so the New Testament, is not one book but a collection of different kinds of writing. These are important because the Church accepted and sanctioned them as its own memory of Jesus, and handed them on as such. St. Augustine once made the point that he would not believe in the Gospels unless the Church had given them to him. The same is true today. When the Church sanctioned these writings in ancient times, it accepted them as they are. They differ from each other. But the Church accepted them as various forms of its own memory of the truth God revealed in Christ for salvation. We have to be able to translate them, to understand their literary forms of expression, and to recognize their differences. Only then will we be able to *read out* of them what the Church accepted as its memory. We must avoid *reading into* them our own ideas or our notions of how to write a book or what the Church should have accepted.[5] We might think of a case where a mother of a family dies and the father sits down with several children to remember her. Each one will come up with memories that are a little different from those offered by the others. But the surviving family accepts the differences in memory as their one larger memory of their mother. So when we ask what the Church actually did say about Mary in the early days, we are asking what the early Church said was its group memory of Mary's role within the story of Jesus that was proclaimed as its religious faith.

From the viewpoint of the second question, when we ask "What does that mean?" about statements of what the early Church actually said about Mary, it will be like asking the father and children of the family used in the example above what they mean by their statements about how they remember their mother. We will have to understand that there is diversity and unity in the memory of the family. Each person's statements will have to be related to the statements of others. Words will have to be understood along with tears or laughter, and not just translated in a dry way. One person's memory will jog another's. Some will remember one event only when another member of the family brings it up. There will be a development of memory as the story goes along. At the end of the discussion the group might make a summary or formal kind of statement about all they have been saying about their mother.

Interpreting statements about Mary made in the New Testament and by teachers in various communities in the early Church will go somewhat along those lines. To see what their statements mean and to get a larger picture of the group memory in the larger growing community of the whole Church we cannot just translate words dryly. We will take into account the symbolic way words were used to express tenderness, respect, reverence and other attitudes. That means we will have to be familiar with the social contexts and symbolic way of thinking in the diverse communities which made up the one Church.[6] We will expect development in memories and differences that eventually help the group to see better what Mary meant as time went on. We will be aware that different biases and turns of phrase are part of human memory. Above all we will take into account that the memory of Mary is part of the "formal summary" or "proclamation"[7] of faith in Jesus the Lord and his story, which the growing Church began to explain further for itself with the help of the Holy Spirit as time went on.[8]

From the viewpoint of the third question—"How did the Church's memory of Mary make Mary present in the Church?"—we will keep in mind that the Church's sacred group memory of Mary was part of the Church's participation in the ongoing mystery of Jesus' salvation for all people. In her memory the Church proclaimed its origin, its meaning in the present, and its direction in the future. This was the "economy of salvation." From the creation God planned that the Son would become human and die and rise for everyone. Those who believe in the Son will always be united to him through the gift of his life to us through the Spirit. The Church proclaimed this in word and ritual, doing what Christ said "in memory of him," thereby opening up to the Spirit to encounter the risen Christ in daily life. As the Church remembered this "mystery" of Christ, Mary was an essential part of it. She was the mother of the Lord, according to God's eternal plan. But she was holy and obedient, and opened herself to the Spirit. She was the virgin mother who said "yes" to God's will. She heard the word and kept it. She persevered in her life of faithful relationship with God and her Son and the Spirit, despite difficulties. The Church remembered her in various communities' prayers and proclamation of the words and deeds of the Lord in this way. Slowly the Church sanctioned the Gospel memories of Mary as the Church's own "formal summary" of Mary. Growing in unity amid the diverse communities, the Church saw Mary as the very type of the Church itself: giving birth to the Lord, model of openness to the Spirit and obedience to the word of God, the new Eve in the new creation.[9]

The group memory of Mary emerged in the Church as the model of the Church's own identity. This was a formative development. The one Church saw in many ways that Mary guaranteed the humanity of the Lord through the incarnation of the Son of God, and that she guaranteed the way that Christ could be present at all times in the believing communities on earth. Remembering Mary's role in the origins of its existence, the Church also took this as part of its memory of the present meaning of itself, and as part of its picture of its mission and goal. The Church saw itself as Mary—mother to Christ in his present life within Christians, open to the Spirit, servant of God in holiness. Mary was present to the Church in the Church's own memory and life through this "recollection." The Church remembered Christ and itself in its proclamation of faith and its rituals. Mary was present deep in its group memory as its self-image. Therefore to study the memory of Mary in order to recapture the Church's memory of her is to enter a kind of introspection and self-discovery. We ask our mother the Church, who is also us, *who we are* when we delve into the presence of Mary in the

Church's memory. We will discover Mary in our own memory. For when we recuperate the memory of Jesus' story for ourselves, and Mary's part in it, we recover our own identity. Then we encounter Christ and Mary as present to us in our sacramental group memory. We celebrate this encounter in our liturgies and remember it as part of ourselves in our daily lives.

As we proceed in the next chapters, then, the fact that the memory of Mary is a part of the sacred group memory of the Church will be the vantage point from which we start. That will color all our thoughts.

REFERENCES

1. More information on this topic can be found in M. Eliade, *Rites and Symbols of Initiation*, translated by W. Trask (New York: Harper and Row, 1965) and in J. Waardenburg, "Symbolic Aspects of Myth," in *Myth, Symbol and Reality*, ed. by A.M. Olson (University of Notre Dame Press, 1980), pp. 41–68.

2. For further basic reading on the critical study of the Bible see B. Rigaux, O.F.M., "Critical History and the Gospels," in *Faith, Reason and the Gospels*, ed. by J. Heaney, S.J. (Westminster: Newman Press, 1963), pp. 211–226; H.C. Kee, *Jesus in History* (New York: Harcourt Brace Jovanovich, 1977), pp. 9–21; R.E. Brown, *The Critical Meaning of the Bible* (New York: Paulist Press, 1981).

3. More information on the very current topic of "hermeneutic" can be found in Francis S. Fiorenza, *Foundational Theology—Jesus and the Church* (New York: Crossroad, 1985), pp. 29–45, 289–311 and in R. North, S.J., "Interpreting the Economy of Salvation: Reconciling Pre-Biblical, Biblical, and Post-Biblical Horizons of Experience," in *Modern Biblical Scholarship: Its Impact on Theology and Proclamation*, edited by F. Eigo (Villanova University Press, 1984), pp. 87–124.

4. For further studies of *anamnesis* (Greek) or *zikkaron* (Hebrew) see C. Vaggaggini, *Theological Dimensions of the Liturgy*, ed. 4, translated by L. Doyle and W. Jergens (Collegeville: Liturgical Press, 1976); J. Emminghaus, *The Eucharist*, translated

by M. O'Connell (Collegeville: Liturgical Press, 1978), pp. 12–19, 45, 74; C.P.M. Jones, "The New Testament," in *The Study of the Liturgy*, ed. by C.P.M. Jones (New York: Oxford University Press, 1978), pp. 148–169; G. Wainwright, "The Understanding of the Liturgy in the Light of Its History," in *The Study of the Liturgy* (cited above), pp. 495–509; and T. Guzie, "The Liturgical Year: What Does It Mean to Remember?" in *The Church Gives Thanks and Remembers*, ed. by L. Johnson (Collegeville: Liturgical Press, 1984), pp. 37–52.

5. Past interpretations of the Scriptures often deter us from reading what is in the text. See A. Dulles, S.J., *A Church To Believe In* (New York: Crossroad, 1982), Chapter 3.

6. On the importance of symbols, as opposed to concepts, see A. Dulles, S.J., "The Symbolic Structure of Revelation," *Theological Studies*, 41/1, March 1980, pp. 51–73, and L. Gilkey, *Catholicism Confronts Modernity* (New York: Seabury Press, 1975), Chapter 3.

7. *Proclamation* is an important category of Church expression. See O. Semmelroth, S.J., *The Preaching Word—On the Theology of Proclamation*, translated by J. Hughes (New York: Herder and Herder, 1965); R.H. Fuller, *The Use of the Bible in Preaching* (Philadelphia: Fortress Press, 1981), pp. 25ff; E. La Verdiere, *The New Testament in the Life of the Church* (Notre Dame: Ave Maria Press, 1980).

8. E. Schillebeeckx, O.P. has studied the relation of Spirit and memory in the work of proclamation of the faith. See his *Ministry—Leadership in the Community of Jesus Christ*, translated by J. Bowden (New York: Crossroad, 1981), pp. 33–38, 135ff. Summaries of his work can be found in J.M. Connolly, *Human History and the Word of God* (New York: Macmillan, 1965), p. 255, and in the work of Fiorenza cited above, pp. 32–39.

9. See O. Semmelroth, S.J., *Mary Archetype of the Church*, translated by M. von Eroes and J. Devlin (New York: Sheed and Ward, 1963), Chapter 2; B. Ahern, C.P., *New Horizons—Studies in Biblical Theology* (Notre Dame: Fides Publishers, 1965), Chapter 10; B. Buby, S.M., "Mary, a Model of *Ecclesia-Orans* in Acts 1:14," in *Marian Studies*, 34, 1984, pp. 87–99.

3

THE MEMORY OF MARY
IN THE SYNOPTIC GOSPELS

"What we have seen and heard . . . " (1 Jn 1:1).
" . . . being no hearer who forgets" (Jas 1:25).

We are the Church. As we recollect our sacred memory of Jesus to recover Mary's part in it, we go back to the Gospel testimonies. We try to regain what we testify to and proclaim by engaging in the work of uncovering the meaning of the Gospel. Our basic memory of Mary is a "scriptural testimony."[1] It is a testimony or witness that brings together the rich symbols of the experience of the early Christians. It is more than what reason alone can say or uncover. It is a testimony of human experience in the clothes of divine faith.[2] It is about the role and meaning of Mary as the early Christians remembered her part in the human history of the divine revelation of Jesus, man and God. The truth of Mary cannot be separated from her meaning in the Gospels. In our interpretation of those Gospels, "meaning cannot be separated from truth."[3] The Gospel communities handed on to us as their "witness" the truth they *knew about* Mary, and her meaning to them as they came to *know* her.

If I had an elderly grandmother, and I asked her about her own grandmother whom she knew long ago when she was a little girl, she would relate to me a treasured family memory. She would tell me what that lady meant to her. And that would be more than all the photographs or objective histories could tell. She would testify to that lady's meaning and role in her life.

That is the kind of memory the Church has of Mary. But the Church has the Holy Spirit to help it not to forget, too. And just as my grandmother would tell me stories, and remember titles of honor (she was "the village beauty," "the hardest worker"), that is the way the people of God recorded Mary: she had meaning for them in the story of Jesus and his accomplishment, and she had precious titles.

Since I cannot talk to the early Christians who composed the Gospels, I, and you, have to rely on critical history to uncover the stories and titles, the personal symbols and testimony, that are in the Gospels. Critical study will give us the testimony, the stories and symbols and titles. But hermeneutics and the other disciplines of today can help us to pierce the meaning of those expressions.

Work has been going on to get to the history and then on to the meaning in the documented history. It is often work that remains in scholarly journals. It cannot stay there. It must be made known to the people at large. Some teachers and preachers have avoided doing this. Maybe it is because they are comfortable with their old ideas or afraid of new ones. Whatever the reason may be, the work of bridging the gap between scholars and people has to start. Otherwise only a former uncritical history will be available to the people—a "life of Mary" with pictures of European ladies painted in the Renaissance, more emotion and aesthetics than Christian memory. Then our people will never get to know the real Mary whom the Church remembered.

To help our family in this task of remembering, nothing is more important than to start with the Gospels. What can we say about the Gospels and Mary's role in them from a critical viewpoint, and with prayerful interpretation?

What Is a Gospel?

Maybe the best place to start in our recollection is to ask what a Gospel is. Not too long ago we "heard the Gospel" at Mass. It was in Latin. We could read the translation in our missal. We also read some "lives" of Christ. If we did any further study it was usually to learn many different biblical quotations which we related to one another without much insight or knowledge, or we found single passages relating to one subject, for example "woman," and put them together in historical order or some other order to relate them to

Mary. Some theologians did much the same thing, but in Latin. We presumed that we knew what a Gospel is.

That has all changed. Not only is the Gospel proclaimed in English in the Mass, but it is done so in such a way that the different Gospels can be heard and considered one after the other. And there are no more "lives of Christ." At least there aren't any that put all the Gospels together as one continuous objective history. And if there are such, there shouldn't be. We understand more about the Gospels today. We know they are not "biographies." What are they?

The four Gospels which the Church claims as its own are four different portraits of who Jesus was and what he did. They are four different memories of the meaning of the history of Jesus. Jesus' life was unique and single. But the oral traditions and liturgical commemorations of the "good news" were multiple. Jesus left his followers his own Spirit to help them remember him and all that he and his accomplishment meant. The Holy Spirit helped them to remember the meaning of Jesus in their own ways. He did not provide them with a TV documentary or a tape recording. Humans always remember real people for their meaning, and try to express in stories, titles, and familiar figures what they remember. That is how the disciples who began to form different communities remembered Jesus.

Each of the four Gospels is a *unique composition* with a *special meaning* or *message* for a particular community of disciples within the Church at large. It is our task to understand both the *composition* and the *meaning*. That is the way we can see how they present Mary's role in their sacred memory of Jesus. She is included in each of the four, but since they are different portraits of Jesus they will give us different portraits of Mary.

Of course there is only one Jesus and one Gospel. But there are four different portraits, four different memories of that one Gospel. That is to be expected from humans. It is the way we remember. And in the case of remembering what is not only human but divine we should expect many different ways of trying to capture what is infinite.

The Church always insisted that different Gospel portraits be expressions of the one Gospel of Christ. Many Gospels were rejected by the Church as inauthentic memories of Jesus and who he was. They are the so-called "apocryphal" Gospels, which did not square with the Church's memory and understanding of Jesus since the time of the preaching of the apostles and eyewitnesses to Jesus' work.

The notion of "Gospel" pertains above all to the preaching and proclamation about Jesus. The authoritative word of Jesus, who fulfilled the Scriptures and hopes of Israel, became the authoritative word of those to whom Jesus gave his Spirit in order to remember his words. The words of the first preachers, especially the eleven and those who had been with him since his baptism by John, were a "testimony." The communities in which they preached remembered these words and incorporated them into their prayer life. They proclaimed them to believers and non-believers. This kind of proclamation of their faith included all the possible ways in which it could be done in the various situations in which communities of believers found themselves.[4] They preached, prayed, meditated, shared reactions, tried to convince others, both Jews and Gentiles. They wrote down collections of Jesus' sayings and various stories that people told about him. Above all it was in their special recollection of the passion, death and resurrection of Jesus, and of his words before that time—in the context of their common or ritual prayers and the breaking of bread—that the particular structure of what we call a "Gospel" developed.

Various Gospels were composed by different communities of believers. They were sacred memories of the apostolic or eyewitness testimonies about Jesus. They were used in community liturgies. Jesus was remembered in word and in sacrament, in story and in ritual, in order to recognize his presence in the community as he had promised. Some communities, as we know from the New Testament itself (for example the letters of Paul and John), fought over different meanings they saw in Jesus. Only when other communities or apostolic eyewitness testimonies from the past took sides was one part of the disagreement "excommunicated." Some communities had produced Gospels which were portraying not the commonly shared meaning of Jesus since the time of the eyewitnesses but a "Gnostic" Jesus, a spirit without human body. These were rejected. Some Gospels were produced which emphasized pious imaginations and curiosities about Jesus as a wonder worker rather than the common traditional Gospel. These were rejected by the other Churches, too. It was not until 1546, at the Council of Trent, that the Church closed the question of the number of writings and Gospels which the whole Church accepted as "canonical" or as a "rule" or "canon" for the Church's sacred memory. But the Church had accepted the four "canonical" Gospels as four different expressions of the true faith by the second century.

Within the writings of the canonical New Testament the Gospels have always had and still hold a priority of importance.[5] They are special compositions of the very *proclamation of faith* which the other New Testament writings presume or refer to only in passing. These are the basic sacred memories of the Church. The Church hands on what it received: the Gospel. The Church celebrates the Gospel in deed by repeating ritually the passion, death, and resurrection of Jesus and proclaiming his words and deeds. This is the liturgy. It is the Gospel in ritual enactment. In liturgy and Scripture the Church remembers and makes present the living Jesus, the Lord. The Church hands on that memory and presence. It uses every symbolic way that is useful to do this. It uses the four portraits of the meaning of the one Jesus in the Gospels. It uses various rites of liturgical expression. It is always looking backward to move forward. The passion, death, and resurrection of Jesus color all the Church's life. The Church even looks backward to before the resurrection: to the baptism and preaching of Jesus, to his infancy, to the fulfillment of the Hebrew Scriptures, and to the eternal plan of God before all time. All of these point to the resurrection, and the resurrection points to now and to the future. This is the story the Church remembers in "Gospel." And Mary is a part of it.

Gospel compositions, then, are not what we would call biographies—the kind you buy in our bookstores today. They do not just deal with the past, and do that critically. They were composed as recitals and proclamations of the sacred memory of what Jesus *meant* to the communities which had received the story of Jesus' words and deeds from eyewitnesses or disciples of eyewitnesses. Writers used narratives and discourses to do this. They composed sacred memories that look backward to the resurrection of Jesus in order to see his meaning for the present time. They portray his meaning by showing that he was God and man. A backward movement or memory is always involved in order to display this meaning. One Gospel moves backward in its picture of Jesus, from his passion, death and resurrection to the beginning of his public preaching at his baptism. Two move backward to his infancy to show how he was the Lord, fulfilling the Hebrew Scriptures, from his conception and birth. One Gospel moves back to the infinity of God before all creation to envision the meaning of Jesus the Divine Word. All of these backward movements involve stories and a message for the present situation of the writers' communities. They enable them to see how the symbolic actions and titles of Jesus give divine strength to people in later times.[6]

One community would use the writings of another community. They would hear preachers from other communities. But always the Gospel meaning was the same. The stories were told a little differently, but this enabled the people to get the message more clearly. By the time the four Gospels were composed, before the end of the first century, the Church at large had a clearly developed memory of Jesus and the salvation he accomplished. Development in clarity came through reflection on one portrait in order to retell the story with more understanding of Jesus through the Church's experience of his presence. Above all the reflection included how Jesus fulfilled the Hebrew Scriptures and had made a whole new creation.

Such was the Gospel faith and memory of the Church, one, yet locally diverse. Its understanding of Jesus developed. By looking backward it was moving forward, under the guidance of the Spirit. It was always careful, as we know from the other writings in the New Testament besides the Gospels, to avoid corruption of the meaning of Jesus handed on from the beginning.

The Church's memory of Jesus included Mary. Her role was understood more clearly as time went on, too. We can see the development of the memory of Mary within the Gospels themselves. The Church preserved this clarified memory with care. Other curiosities about Mary were written down—some of them, like her parents' names, are with us today—but the Church never made them part of its authentic Gospel memory. What it preserved in the Gospels as its memory of Mary we will turn to now.

The Development of the Gospel Memory of Mary

We know from historical study that the Gospel of Mark was the first of the four Gospels to be composed. Both Matthew and Luke depended on Mark as a source for their Gospel compositions. These three Gospels differ very much from the portrait of John's Gospel. The meaning is the same. It is the one Gospel handed down from the beginning of the Church. But the one Gospel is synopsized by Mark in brief. Matthew and Luke follow the same synopsis in general, adding their own insights. (These three are called the Synoptic Gospels.) John takes a wholly different approach to his composition. He portrays the same Gospel with deep theology and reflection upon the Hebrew Scriptures and the experience of the Church. He is more poetic in his use of symbols. His composition allows the meaning of Jesus to become much clearer.

There is not a great deal about Mary in the first three Gospels. However there is enough to make even the most critical student of the Gospels raise an eyebrow in surprise when he or she reads statements like the one of John McKenzie that "the genuine historical evidence about Mary is so slight as to impose upon the historian, were anyone else concerned, an embarassed silence."[7] McKenzie is talking about "historical evidence." If that means a biographic knowledge in our sense of biography, he should know better than to look for that in the Gospels. So should "the historian." The Gospels offer a sacred memory, a testimony, a proclamation in story form, and Mary has a great deal of meaning in them. That is the historical memory of the early Christians: a memory of her role and meaning within their belief about Jesus the Lord. The first three Gospels may not say much about her, but they testify, in their few remarks, to her special importance. We know that from hermeneutic study of them.

Where Mary is recalled in the Synoptic Gospels she is described as a very important person in the story of Jesus and his meaning for Christians in the present. It is not a matter of *how many words* are written about her. It is a question of her meaning in the composition. We will look at her meaning in each of the three Synoptic Gospels. In the next chapter we will look at how the Gospel of John remembers her meaning and role in the story of Jesus.

The Gospel of Mark

It is true that the Gospel of Mark has extremely little to say about Mary. What he does say is rather negative—a point that Matthew and Luke will change. He insists that Mary is not important merely because she is the blood mother of Jesus. Only a spiritual relationship to Jesus is important. (That is the point that the other two Gospels will develop.) It is important to keep this in mind, and the fact that the other Gospels have to be taken into account, for ecumenical discussions. Mark's Gospel has been the favorite Gospel of Protestant Christians, while Matthew's Gospel was the most read in Catholic liturgies for a long time. Matthew adds to Mark. So does Luke. Our Protestant brothers and sisters should remember that. Catholics should understand that a preference for Mark has influenced Protestant estimation of Mary.[8]

Mark's Gospel is a remembrance of how the Lord who suffered and died and rose for us was abandoned. Jesus had to upbraid his disciples for their unbelief even after his resurrection. Mark wants, in this stark portrait, to remind the Church of the difficulty of being a disciple. To be the true family of Jesus, the new sons and daughters of the Father, the "eschatological family" of the kingdom of God, is a hard challenge. The only true family of Jesus in the kingdom is made up of those who are related to Jesus by dedicated faith which is proven by bearing the cross.

In this portrayal he presents the stories and words of Jesus before his death as a reminder of the challenge. In the third chapter (as we divide up the Gospel, not as Mark did) we read that Jesus was doing so many good things for so many people that crowds surrounded him and almost crushed him. Jesus keeps on doing good for the people even though they do not show much faith. Jesus goes from the lake country over to the hill country. He goes into a house. The crowd even follows him into the house. It even became impossible to eat. People started to say he was overworking.

At this point Jesus' family comes to the house. They want to take charge of him. They evidently thought he was just working too hard and "killing himself." They were not putting the work of the kingdom of God first as Jesus was doing.

Before they arrived at the house, however, Mark makes it his business to tell us how the religious establishment used the situation. They accuse Jesus of being crazy, of acting like a person possessed. Mark reminds the community for whom he wrote that Jesus has no patience with that kind of attitude. Jesus refutes the religious establishment. He accuses them of not listening to the Holy Spirit. (Certainly that was a message for Mark's church community.) It is after this that the mother and brothers and sisters of Jesus arrive.

Notice how Mark portrays Jesus' blood relatives. They think they will take over because they are his family. But they stay outside the house while the people who listen to Jesus' words are inside the house. His relatives send him a message asking him to come out to them. What a portrait! They send a message to the messenger of God. They tell him they know what is best for him. They think that being his blood family is evidence enough that they know better than he does what is good.

Jesus replies by speaking to those inside the house who were listening to him. (For Mark's community the message is also to listen to the Holy Spirit in the house of the Lord's word.) He says that his "true" mother and brother and sister are those who listen to him, those who do the will of God. The new family of God in the kingdom is to be made up of those who believe in him because they listen to the word of God.

The point for Mark and his readers is that discipleship is a matter of faith. The Church, the brothers and sisters of Jesus who are adopted children of God, co-heirs with Christ, is not the natural relationship of family. Mark does not say someone couldn't be both—a natural relative of Jesus and a faith relative. He does put Mary and Jesus' relatives by blood outside the circle of hearers of the word, however, to make his point.

Mark does the same thing with regard to Jesus' neighborhood acquaintances. In the sixth chapter he tells us about Jesus and his disciples on a trip to Jesus' home town. The people who knew Jesus as he grew up and who knew his relatives react negatively to the word. They have only natural knowledge of Jesus and natural expectations, rather than faith. Jesus is taken aback. He hoped that they would have moved from natural familiarity to a faith relationship. But they didn't. Jesus is abandoned. He could not work any miracles, works of faith, among those acquaintances. Being a neighbor of Jesus, someone who knew him from his birth, counts for nothing in the kingdom unless that person has faith.

Mark's own community got the message. Even the disciples and apostles of Jesus, who knew him in his preaching days, had to be upbraided for their lack of faith after the resurrection. Only that faith which lasts even to the point of dying for others will make someone a member of the family of God in the kingdom. (See Mk 3:21,31–35; 6:1–6; 10:28–31,43–45; 16:14.)

Mark's memory of Jesus emphasizes the difficulty of discipleship. It is more than a natural relationship or acquaintanceship with Jesus. He remembers Mary as the natural mother of Jesus. Being the natural mother of Jesus does not make her a member of the kingdom family. He does not say that she was not more than a natural relative of Jesus. He uses her natural maternity as an example of blood relationship. But he does not say that Mary was more than the blood mother of Jesus, either.

The Gospel of Matthew

When Matthew composed his Gospel he used Mark's Gospel as one of his sources of the Church memory of Jesus. He used other sources, too. He changed some of Mark's meanings in order to benefit his own community and to clarify the meaning of Jesus. The meaning of Mary and her role in the kingdom is one of the things he changed.

The Christians for whom Matthew wrote his Gospel had strong Jewish traditions. We can also see from the way Matthew composed his stories and put them together in a narrative memory that the group was undergoing special difficulties which threatened to divide them into splinter groups. Some of the problems had to do with their relation to their Jewish background, the influence of new members, and wandering prophets. Matthew underscored the pointed meaning that the disciples of Jesus have to be people who avoid scandal and become reconciled with each other. That is what being a disciple demands.

In his memory of Mary he makes changes in Mark's story about Mary and the relatives of Jesus, and he prefaces the whole Gospel with an infancy Gospel.

In 12:46–50 and 13:53–58 he repeats Mark's episodes about Jesus' mother, relatives, and neighbors. He softens the whole message. Jesus' family does not come to take charge of Jesus because of a rumor that he has been overworking. He removes the "inside-outside" distinction between the place of Jesus' blood relatives and the place of those who are listening to Jesus' words. Matthew simply says that the family came looking for Jesus. He has Jesus then say that his family in the new kingdom are his disciples, those who hear the word of God. Jesus' message is that faith, not natural blood relationship, makes one a member of the "eschatological" family, the adopted children of God. Jesus points to those who are there listening to him, to emphasize the difference between faith and blood.

Why this softening of the message that was in Mark? Because Matthew, as we shall see, and Luke in both his Gospel and the Acts of the Apostles, are aware of a larger Church memory about Mary and James the "brother" of the Lord. From within Matthew's Gospel we see that the very way he composes his memories gives a reason for his softening. He not only remembers the passion, death and resurrection of Jesus, and the words and deeds of Jesus' public life beginning with God's approval of Jesus as his Son at Jesus' baptism. He looks even further backward to the infancy of Jesus. Jesus was the Son of God, the fulfillment of Israel's hope and promises, from his conception and birth. And in the composition of this preface to the public manifestation of Jesus as man and God, he includes the memory of Mary as a woman with a special relationship to the Holy Spirit and the coming of the kingdom.

We don't write prefaces like "infancy Gospels" today. These creative compositions (Luke has one too) are special kinds of literary forms of writing which spell out what St. Paul insisted was a part of Christian faith. St. Paul puts it very succinctly in the letter he wrote to the Christians of Galatia. Jesus was "born of a woman, born under the law." Jesus really existed as a human and as a Jew. Jesus was man, as well as God. And Mary was the instrument God used in the mystery of sending his Son to take on human flesh, a mystery planned by God out of love for us from all eternity.

In Matthew's infancy preface he used an old way of getting a message across, a way his Jewish community appreciated more than we do. He gave a genealogy. Luke used a genealogy, too. But Matthew placed his at the beginning of the infancy stories which he tells, while Luke placed his genealogy at the beginning of the public adult life of Jesus. The list of names differs, too. Matthew includes Mary. Luke does not. In fact, the two genealogies differ in their very purpose and meaning. Here we will examine Matthew's genealogy along with his infancy narratives. When we look at Luke's compositions we will better appreciate the difference and the development between the meaning and memory in the two Gospels.

Matthew's Gospel recalls the meaning of Jesus for a community that was very concerned with the Jewish law. It portrays Jesus as the fulfillment of Israel's law and prophets. Jesus is the new Moses, a law-giver. He is a new king of Israel, a new David. He is the promised Emmanuel, the presence of God with his people. In his genealogy Matthew shows that Jesus is in the line of Abraham and is a son of David. David's town of Bethlehem is the place of Jesus' human origin. Jesus is born of Mary, a Jewish mother. Joseph provides the lineage of David in a legal way. He is not the father of Jesus, for Mary, in fulfillment of the prophecy in Isaiah 7:14, conceives Jesus virginally, by the power of the Holy Spirit.

We can see how this meant so much to Matthew's fellow Christians. They believe in the one Gospel. They are looking backward from the resurrection and the gift of the Holy Spirit to the Church, back to the birth of Jesus. The Holy Spirit brought about the birth of the promised Savior, just as the Holy Spirit brings about the life of the Church. Mary is placed in a relationship with the Holy Spirit the way these people knew that they were in relationship with the Spirit. She is the acme of Israel in its relationship with God.[9]

God fulfills his promise to Israel, his promise to Mary, and his promise to the Church through the Holy Spirit. This is what God, through an angel, tells Joseph, "a just man." Joseph is a guardian of the hope of Israel.

The divine meaning of Jesus is told in the story form of the announcement of the angel to Joseph. Who is Jesus? He is the promised Savior and "God with us." He is the One who will rise from the dead and be with the Church forever. All the prophets pointed to this Jesus. His name and titles show this (see 5:17; 18:20; 28:20). His salvation is for all people. The story of the magi shows this. Only those who lack faith, who are not true Israelites, like Herod, reject Jesus' salvation. But even the Egyptians can be saved. As the Jews once were enslaved in Egypt, but were delivered by God, so now the Savior finds refuge in Egypt. This is the gift to all that God had promised. Moses was the prophet who brought Israel out of Egypt, but the Son of God is a new Moses who will now save Egyptians and all people. The pharaoh tried to kill Moses as a baby.

Herod is the one who would kill the new infant Moses. God preserved Moses in Egypt. He preserved his Son from Herod. All that happened to Moses in the time of the law is a type of Jesus, giver of the new law on a new mount.[10] All that the Jews hoped for and were promised is fulfilled in this child. Even Nazareth, his home town, is part of the fulfillment.

Even though Matthew tells stories which portray Jesus' meaning as the Savior and new Moses, his memory includes Mary and Joseph. He portrays their meaning. Joseph is a guardian, a just man who preserved the hope of Israel. Mary is the woman who was so related to the Holy Spirit that she was the one who became the mother of Jesus, the Son of God. No wonder that Matthew softened the Markan story about Mary. She was more than a name and the blood mother of Jesus. She is the virgin mother of Israel, promised sign of the Messiah.[11] She provides the possibility of Israel's hope, the presence of God with them. Therefore when Matthew comes to the public life of Jesus, before the passion, death and resurrection, he sees Mary not only in the opposition between blood relationship to Jesus and faith relationship to Jesus, but as the woman whose role in the new law was special. She is not called a disciple of Jesus. But she is more than just his natural mother. She is the Jewish woman who was special in her relationship to God and in God's plan of salvation. She is the hoped-for and promised virgin mother.

Is Matthew describing facts? What is a fact? Facts are events insofar as they have meaning. The year 1066 and the battle of Hastings have a meaning—the French-Norman conquest of England which changed English history in many ways. Therefore 1066 is one of the "facts" of history. Matthew presents the fact of the birth of Jesus in its meaning. The Lord, risen from the dead, was the fulfillment of Israel's hope from his birth as a human Jew. This is the meaning of Jesus' birth, and Matthew remembers it in terms of God's symbols of promise in the Hebrew Scriptures. Mary is a part of his portrait of the meaning of Jesus. Her meaning as more than the mere blood mother of Jesus is recalled, too.

The Gospel of Luke

When Luke composed his Gospel he, too, softened and changed Mark's picture of Mary. He did it for Christians who were not in the same situation as Matthew's readers. His intended audience was less Jewish, more Hellenistic in their cultural ways, and very interested in the theology of discipleship. The sacred memory of Jesus which he composed and recorded for the group to read and celebrate is a portrait of the one Gospel in terms of Jesus as the kind and merciful Savior of all people, the human and divine Lord who gives his spirit to all men and women of every race through his disciples. He composed both the Gospel and the Acts of the Apostles to tell the story of Jesus and his disciples. These should be taken as complementary: the story of the passion, death and resurrection of Jesus and how he made disciples and was present with them through the Spirit even after his return to the Father.

Mary is remembered in Luke's compositions before and after the central event of Jesus' passion, death and resurrection. She is part of the story of Jesus' public ministry, part of the preface about Jesus' infancy, and part of the story of the post-resurrection community.

In his telling of the sacred memory of Jesus' public ministry, Luke repeats Mark's episodes about Jesus' mother and relatives and neighbors (4:16–30; 8:19–21). Like Matthew, he changes them. But he does so from his own theological explanation of the meaning of Jesus for the readers of his Gospel. He omits the contrast between blood relatives and disciples. He tells how Jesus' mother and relatives looked for Jesus. They could not get to him because of the crowd. Jesus is told that they are "outside"—that is, all that is left of Mark's inner circle inside the house as opposed to those who are not inside the house. Jesus replies that those who hear the word of God and keep it are his mothers and relatives, without any gesture of pointing to the circle around him.

Now Luke has taken great care, with precise language, to distinguish "crowd" from "disciples." So he does not separate Jesus' mother from his disciples, but from the crowd. This was important for the Church community for whom the Gospel was written. They were very interested in hearing about Jesus and what discipleship meant. Luke is aware of this. He adds an episode in the public ministry about Mary and discipleship to explain his intention. In chapter 11, verses 27 and 28, a woman is described in the act of shouting a macharism or blessing for Jesus' mother: "Blessed is the womb that bore you." She is referring to Jesus' natural mother. Jesus replies to the woman that what would be a correct blessing would be to say: Blessed are they who hear the word of God and keep it. And that is the exact beatitude which Luke applied to Mary already in the Gospel (1:45,49). His point is that Mary is not to be excluded from the disciples. She is not a "disciple" of Jesus, as that is used of others in Christian memory. She is never listed among disciples. But she is a special "hearer of the word of God" who kept that word. So she is to be blessed, even though it is not because she is only the blood mother of Jesus. She was a special blood mother, full of faith. That is why Luke does not separate her from the disciples in his retelling of Mark's story. His memory of Mary's meaning had already been told in his preface, the infancy narratives. Here he changes Mark to keep that memory of Mary. In the Acts of the Apostles he will place her with the disciples in the first community of the post-resurrection church (1:14).

The infancy stories of Luke differ from those of Matthew. He does not include a genealogy among them. He does have a genealogy at the beginning of the stories of the public ministry. In that composition he shows that Jesus is the Savior of all people, since Jesus' ancestry is traced back to Adam. Matthew's Jewish interests had traced Jesus back to Abraham. The same meaning of Jesus—his universal healing—is the background for the infancy stories and for the Acts of the Apostles. The prophecy of Isaiah about the suffering servant of Yahweh who is a light for all the nations is always in Luke's mind as he composes (Lk 1:54; 24:27; Acts 4:27).

How does Luke look backward from the resurrection and public life to the infancy of Jesus to show that Jesus was Lord of all from the first moments of his human existence? The child Jesus is portrayed as light to the nations, Savior to the poor, new presence of God's wisdom in the temple. Luke's "Christology," his explanation of the meaning of Jesus as Christ and Lord, colors his infancy stories.

He begins his preface to the public life of Jesus, who died and rose, with a very artistic double comparison: the Old Testament is compared to the New, and John the Baptist is compared to Jesus. He presents Mary as having a special role in the new salvation of Jesus.

The first thing Luke does is draw a parallel between the conception and birth of the Baptist and those of Jesus. The difference between his picture of the meaning of Jesus and that of Matthew is evident from the first. Here there is no annunciation to Joseph, no visit of the magi, no mention of Egypt or the slaughter of the innocent children by Herod. Whatever he shares with Matthew is changed to suit his portrait of the birth of the same risen Lord. He uses other sources, too, and cleverly adapts other pictures from the Hebrew Scriptures than the stories of Moses, in order to show another side of the meaning of the human Jesus who was also the saving Lord. Luke is not writing what we call a biography. And when he speaks of Mary he is not writing a life of Mary, nor even interested in the curiosities with which the apocryphal "gospels" like the *Protogospel of James* are filled. His picture of Mary is contained in his picture of Jesus. He remembers her meaning for a faithful people. We have to read out of his stories the picture of Mary "according to Luke" with care to avoid the temptation to read into this Gospel a picture of Mary "according to our expectations."

The comparison between Jesus and John the Baptist starts with an angelic announcement[12] to John's father Zechariah in the temple where he performs the institutional religious duties of the priestly caste. The story of John follows. Paralleled with the annunciation of a heavenly messenger of God, a symbol of divine revelation, to Zechariah in his formal temple situation is the sudden announcement of God's message to a humble virgin girl in her home in a small town—the memorable annunciation to Mary. It would be good to try to remember all the details which have been painted into our memories by artists of the Renaissance, in order to push them out of our sight—not that they are not beautiful testimonies from that particular time, but because of what they miss. Luke is comparing the old and the new, the institutional temple and the humble way of the new Lord of the temple, fear and joy. There are no gold trappings in the Gospel portrait. The girl is the one favored with God's very special love. She is the beginning of messianic joy. She does not react with fear; she is told not to fear. The fear of God's presence, a traditional Jewish symbolic way of picturing the awesome aspect of God's glory, is replaced with the joy that gives a new kind of glory to God—the resurrection of the Lord is "good news" for all. Men were usually the recipients of God's message in Israel; here is a woman.

The temple was the most sacred place in Israel; here it is wherever Jesus is that is the most sacred place. Mary is the sign of the new way of the Lord.

The power of the word is taken away from Zechariah since he lacks faith. He does not believe that God will make his barren wife Elizabeth a mother, despite the Hebrew knowledge that God had done this in the past with the wives of Abraham, Manoah, and Elkanah. The power of joyful word and song is given to Mary who believes that she has conceived by the power of the Holy Spirit. The words of praise she sings are taken from the praises sung in the Hebrew Scriptures—her Magnificat sums up the praises of women and men who had received God's promises in olden times and who looked to the future, especially the praises of Hannah, the barren woman who received the gift of a son, Samuel, and the praises of the psalms and of the seer of the new covenant, Isaiah. The new sums up the old and is more marvelous. Not the removal of barrenness, but a virginal conception, like a new creation, is the way God has given the gift of his own Son in the final times. Mary is given the title of "woman filled with God's loving favor" and is told to rejoice. Zechariah was only called by his name.

The children's meaning is paralleled by Luke, too. The son of Zechariah and Elizabeth will be called John. He is named in the old way, despite his special meaning. Mary's son will be given the titles that sum up all of the hopes of Israel: great, Son of David, Savior, Son of God. Jesus will be the salvation of God for all as the universal king, by God's will, not because of his legal lineage through Joseph. His Gospel will be different. It will be the gift of the Spirit, who has been present in this whole parallelism, and who has moved the old covenant into the new. John belongs to the old dispensation. (See Lk 3:16–18; 5:33–39.) Jesus brings an entirely new way, the fulfillment of the promise of mercy to the poor (2:15; 4:18).

Now all of this, and more, happens in the two chapters before John and Jesus are compared at the beginning of the adult public life of Jesus. What an artist Luke is. How symbolic and meaningful is the portrait he paints of the infant Lord who rose from the dead, and Mary's role in the beginning of the story of salvation.

Mary's memory is further portrayed in Luke's preface. While

Zechariah had prayed for a son, Mary is simply chosen. She believes whereas he doubts. He stops speaking; Mary spreads the word. She carries the word to Elizabeth, in the mountain country, like the bearers of God's word in Isaiah 52. She brings the unborn Jesus and the Holy Spirit to Elizabeth and the unborn John. The infant John leaps for joy in Elizabeth's womb. Elizabeth, who as a woman fares better as a believer than the man Zechariah—a point which Luke emphasizes about women and discipleship throughout his Gospel—calls Mary "blessed" because she believed. She calls Mary "mother of my Lord," and "Lord" is the title of the risen Jesus. As a woman of faith Elizabeth, and her Spirit-gifted son, John, are special bridges between the old and the new covenants. Zechariah is of the old temple and old ways, and doubts. Mary comes from the old but is the very beginning of the new way. She symbolizes the Church, God's servant, who spreads the word to those who will respond in baptism that "Jesus is Lord," as Luke will describe the Church in Acts.

Luke remembers Mary as the servant of God, filled with the Holy Spirit, full of faith, spreader of the word, joyful mother of the Lord. All ages will call her "blessed," special in her role. For Luke all Christians are called to be servants of God (Acts 3:12–26; 4:29–31). This service of God differs from the service of God in the old dispensation. Mary personifies and describes what service of God means in terms of what Jesus himself said (Lk 6:20ff). She says in her song of praise that this is the fulfillment of the servanthood of Israel (1:54). Zechariah had sung, too. But the service he spoke about was that which led to the hope of the new age which his son John heralded. By comparison Mary exemplifies what it means to be a servant in the new order. [13]

The presence of the Holy Spirit is emphasized in every part of Luke's preface. The Holy Spirit has come to Zechariah and to Elizabeth and to John, as well as to Mary. This is the Holy Spirit which Luke insists is the special gift of the Lord which the old dispensation, symbolized at its best by the baptism of John, could not give. In the Acts of the Apostles the Spirit is the sign of the last days, the new way (2:17; 9:2). Luke's composition of the sacred memory of the Church about the story of Jesus shows the Spirit coming in anticipation before Jesus gives the Spirit, and then the Church inspired by the Spirit to spread that gift of the Spirit to all people. He adds something to our memory of Mary in this way of composing the memory of Jesus.

Mary's relationship to the Spirit, in the preface to the Gospel, is archetypal. She is chosen. She says "yes," the way Jesus will say "yes" to God. The Spirit works wonders through her that are above all the wonders of the old ways—priests, temple, barren women, prophets. Above all, the Holy Spirit works the wonder of the incarnation of the man Jesus who will be seen as Lord. Luke adds two temple stories and a story about the youth of Jesus to his preface to underscore this. These stories are not simply "wondrous child" stories. They are rather in the line of what the Jews called "midrash," perhaps like "mashal." But they are not exactly that kind of story, either. They do not comment on texts. They are not literature about literature the way those Jewish forms of storytelling were. Rather they are prefatory by hindsight. [14] They tell us how the wonder of the incarnation has to be understood in the light of the passion, death and resurrection of Jesus. They show how the passion, death and resurrection of Jesus, the "good news," relate to the former covenant God made with his people, and they do this in terms of Jesus' own words and deeds rather than in terms of Old Testament fulfillment.

The two temple stories tell the community that the new presence of God is recognized by true prophets. The old notion of the temple is changed by the new divine presence (see Acts 5:20; 7:48). The revelation of the risen Lord overshadows the temple. Simeon is a true prophet. He recognizes the new revelation. Moved by the Spirit, he praises God for the new revelation "to the Gentiles," a reference by Luke back to the servant of Yahweh theology of Isaiah. That servant was rejected by many, as well as accepted. The same will happen to Jesus. Luke depicts Mary in a state of wonder at these words about the cross and resurrection of Jesus. Jesus will be rejected. The choice of a disciple is to accept him or to reject him. To accept him is to carry a cross, too (Lk 9:23–27). Simeon tells Mary that a sword will pierce her soul, too. Luke uses the image of the "sword of discrimination" from the Old Testament. The word of God is like a "two-edged sword," as the writer of the Letter to the Hebrews puts it. For Luke the same idea unites Mary and discipleship and the Holy Spirit. Mary, the woman who said "yes" to the word and work of the Holy Spirit, will face the constant challenge of acceptance or rejection. She will have to realize constantly the difference between being Jesus' blood mother and being a woman of faith (Lk 12:51–53). She will persist in faith after the cross and resurrection of Jesus so that she will be with the disciples in the scene in Acts 1:14. But *her* role of facing the cross is singled out. She keeps the message of the Holy Spirit in mind at all times. She reflects on the meaning of Jesus and the new revelation. She puts the meanings of old and new together (Luke calls her "symbolousa" in Greek, which means "putting the symbolic meanings together"). He mentions this characteristic of Mary three times (2:19,33,51).

Why does Luke so describe Mary, with a sword-pierced heart? He certainly does not describe her in the way some artists have, as pierced with the sword of Jesus' death and suffering at the foot of the cross. However, those conflations of Luke's explanation of Mary's meaning and the one in the Gospel of John—which we will see in the next chapter—are not far from the truth. They only lack the special insights of Luke. His presentation of Mary and the cross is in a wholly different composition. He has Simeon say that the purpose of the sword ("of discrimination") in Mary's inner heart is that "the thoughts of many minds be laid bare." What does that mean? It means that to encounter the mystery of Jesus the risen Lord and servant of Yahweh will always be a challenge. People who hear the word will always either turn away or accept the challenge of discipleship. Luke repeats exactly this theme at the end of the story of the spread of the Church in Acts 28:24–28. There it is Paul who says that this is the way of choice which the Holy Spirit inspired Isaiah to describe with regard to the suffering servant. Paul finds that there are always hearers of the word who accept it, and those who reject it. In the first temple story, then, Luke uses the same theme. The Holy Spirit offers the choice of acceptance or rejection of Jesus the Lord, the light to the Gentiles. Mary is the archetype singled out as the kind of person who accepts the choice of Jesus and the cross.

The second temple story builds upon the first. Its point is how Mary found Jesus, or the manner in which she accepted the choice offered by the Holy Spirit. In this story Jesus appears in the temple when he is twelve years old as the wisdom of God (see 2:46). He fulfills the wisdom of the law and temple. Those who are wise in the law listen to him. They are struck with "wonder." They have the choice. The sword is at work. Mary and Joseph are described as facing this challenge, too. When they seek Jesus in a natural way, only as his kin, only among his neighbors and acquaintances, they do not find him. Blood relationship and neighborhood acquaintance do not make anyone able to enter the kingdom of God by finding the new wisdom. Jesus tells Mary and Joseph that he is not about their business, but about "his Father's work." He will not be found the way humans are found, nor merely by the customary wisdom of the law. Mary and Joseph are struck with "wonder"; they hear his word. They find him the only way he can truly be found as the wisdom of God from the Father, on "the third day." They are like the disciples on the way to Emmaus who, on the third day, recognize Jesus in the new breaking of bread as the redeemer of Israel, and whose hearts move from foolishness to fire as they hear the word of Jesus.

This is a temple story about Jesus the Lord and wisdom of God. It explains scenes in the public ministry where Jesus teaches in the temple and is rejected (20:1–8). Mary has a special role in this memory of Jesus and what he means for disciples. She is described in terms of Luke's special theology. She who was already portrayed in the previous stories as the faithful servant of the Lord, joyful virgin highly favored by God, mother of the Lord by the power of the Holy Spirit to whom she said "yes," proclaimer of God's fulfillment of his promise of mercy to Abraham's children forever, bridge of the old and new covenants who brings the Spirit to the holy people of the old law who listen to the word, even John the Baptist, is presented here as the model of Christian discipleship.

Interestingly, Mary is never called a disciple of Jesus. She is their model, and is described as *along with* the disciples after the resurrection. There is a reason for this juxtaposition. She who found Jesus in the temple on "the third day" exemplifies that Israel who is faithful and receives the Spirit. Like Zion, she is daughter, virgin, and mother.[15] She shows how the old law and old creation can open up to the new law, the new creation. She exemplifies how Israel, the mother of the faithful, changes to the Church, the mother of Jesus' faithful. She is the model of the servanthood and maternity of the Church in its relationship, or, better, our relationship, to the Holy Spirit. She portrays how the Jews can respond to Jesus the Lord and bring the Holy Spirit to others. This is her multifaceted role, her symbolic meaning, the truth about her that we must remember[16]—not the details of her physique or her daily life, but her place in the plan of God.

We can see from these reflection on Luke, in comparison to Mark and to Matthew, that there was a development in the Gospel memory of Mary. The Church, with the guidance of the Holy Spirit, preserved her sacred memory in special written compositions, and constantly reflected upon the meaning of the one Gospel. Like Mary, the Church "kept these things in her heart." It gave us the Gospels. It gave us the meaning of Jesus the Lord, and of Mary, with developed understanding of that meaning.

If we return for a moment to the remark of John McKenzie cited above, we can say that here there is no "embarrassed silence." Here in the memory of the Church we do not find the "historian" in today's sense of that word. We find the depth of history instead. We find the meaning with which "everyone else, including the historian, is concerned."

REFERENCES

1. Mary T. Malone, *Who Is My Mother? Rediscovering the Mother of Jesus* (Dubuque: Wm. C. Brown Co., 1984), p. 32.

2. For more information on "testimony" in critical study of the Gospels see the work of F. Fiorenza, cited previously, pp. 30, 311.

3. *Ibid.* p. 290.

4. See R.E. Brown, *The Churches the Apostles Left Behind* (Ramsey: Paulist Press, 1984).

5. For more information on how the four Gospels became "canonical," see Paul Neuenzeit, "Canon of Scripture," in *Encyclopedia of Theology—The Concise Sacramentum Mundi*, ed. by K. Rahner, S.J. (New York: Seabury Press, 1975), pp. 108–113. See also Vatican II's *Constitution on Divine Revelation*, art. 18, in the edition of Flannery already cited, p. 760.

6. The study of the titles of Jesus is important in Christology. The notion that titles are capsules of theology that are symbolic or

concrete functional summaries of understanding has become standard in historical studies.

7. John McKenzie, "The Mother of Jesus in the New Testament," in *Mary and the Churches*, ed. by H. Küng and J. Moltmann (New York: Seabury Press, 1983), p. 9.

8. See R.E. Brown, "Mary in the New Testament Writings," *America*, May 15, 1982; A.J. Tambasco, *What Are They Saying About Mary?* (Ramsey: Paulist Press, 1984), pp. 26–33; B. Buby, S.M., *Mary, the Faithful Disciple* (Ramsey: Paulist Press, 1985), pp. 18–23.

9. See R.E. Brown *et al.*, *Mary in the New Testament* (Philadelphia: Fortress Press, 1978), pp. 73–103.

10. See J.D. Crossan, "From Moses to Jesus: Parallel Themes," *The Bible Review*, 2/2, Summer 1986, pp. 18–27.

11. See F.J. Moloney, S.D.B., *Woman—First Among the Faithful* (Notre Dame: Ave Maria Press, 1986), p. 47; R.E. Brown, *The Birth of the Messiah* (New York: Doubleday, 1979), pp. 45–46, and *The Virginal Conception and Bodily Resurrection of Jesus* (New York: Paulist Press, 1973), pp. 21–68, and *Mary in the New Testament*, already cited, pp. 83–97, 205 (especially p. 96).

12. On the significance of the symbol of an "announcing angel" see J.A. Fitzmeyer, S.J., *The Gospel According to Luke, I–IX* (New York: Doubleday, 1981), Anchor Bible, Vol. 28, pp. 316, 318, 327, 328.

13. See R.J. Karris, O.F.M., "Mary's Magnificat and Recent Study," *Review for Religious*, 42/6, November 1983, pp. 903–908; J. Dupont, O.S.B., *The Salvation of the Gentiles*, translated by J. Keating, S.J. (New York: Paulist Press, 1979), p. 31.

14. See A.G. Wright, S.S., *Midrash* (New York: Alba House, 1967), pp. 139–142; R.E. Brown, *An Adult Christ at Christmas—Essays on the Three Biblical Christmas Stories* (Collegeville: Liturgical Press, 1978).

15. For Old Testament references in Luke's memory of Mary see R. Russell, O.S.B., "The Blessed Virgin Mary in the Bible,"

in *Mary's Place in Christian Dialogue,* ed. by A. Stacpoole, O.S.B. (Wilton: Morehouse-Barlow Co., 1983), pp. 45–50. Also see J. Cheryl Exum, "The Mothers of Israel," *The Bible Review,* 2/1, 1986, pp. 60–67.

16. To say that Mary is a "member of the Church" or that she meets the criteria for discipleship (*Mary in the New Testament,* cited above, pp. 162, 172) is not to say that Mary was a disciple of Jesus. That could have been said simply by Luke, but it wasn't. Rather she is a disciple of God and a bridge between the old and new dispensations. She is placed along with the disciples in Acts as a model. She belongs to the kingdom of God because of her holiness, not because of her blood maternity of Jesus. John's Gospel remembers her as mother of the disciples. Her place in the Church is more than discipleship, even perfect discipleship. To speak of her as a disciple of Jesus, even a perfect one, seems to be not a critical reading of the New Testament. It also obviates the understanding of the early Church's understanding of Mary as type of the Church as mother, and the Church's memory of Mary in Old Testament figures which she recapitulates. See the way this is handled in P. Bearsley, "Mary the Perfect Disciple: A Paradigm for Mariology," in *Theological Studies,* 41 (1980), pp. 461–504, and in A. Carr, B.V.M., "Mary in the Mystery of the Church: Vatican Council II," in *Mary According to Women,* ed. by C.F. Jegen, B.V.M. (Kansas City: Leaven Press, 1985), pp. 25–26 and note 52. Also see the works of B. Buby and F.J. Moloney already cited. The Jewishness of Mary is yet to be studied in depth, but see David Flusser, "Mary and Israel," in *Mary—Images of the Mother of Jesus in Jewish and Christian Perspective* by J. Pelikan, D. Flusser, and J. Lang (Philadelphia: Fortress Press, 1986), pp. 7–17.

4

MARY IN THE GOSPEL OF JOHN— A DIFFERENT MEMORY

The Gospel of John preserves the *sacred history* of Jesus in a different way from that in the Synoptic Gospels. That is because it is the sacred memory of a different group or Christian community within the one universal Church. The early Church was more aware than we are of local differences that made for diversity within unity.[1] St. Paul wrote to the Corinthian community that they were "called to be saints together with all those who in every place call on the name of the Lord Jesus Christ, both their Lord and ours" (1 Cor 1:2).

We must get used to this idea again in our day. Upon reflection we can see that there is no contradiction between one Gospel and many ways to remember it, or one Church and various local expressions of the faith. Of course each different community expression must be based on what the universal Church recognizes as the "one Lord, one faith, one baptism" proclaimed by the apostles and eyewitnesses whose memories were aided by the Holy Spirit.

Think about it. How do *events* become *history?* Isn't everything that ever happened a part of history? It is true that we cannot remember *everything* that ever happened, even in our own life. And there are some things we never know, even about what happened to us. We cannot remember what we never knew. Then there are some things that just aren't worth remembering, we say. But that is what makes *events* become *history*—that we remember them.

Now our memories are very selective. We remember what was meaningful to us. For example, if I and my brothers and sisters sit down to remember our mother who died, each of us has a little different memory. She meant something very special to each one of us. Each of our memories is about her, and each memory is true. But they differ from each other.

The same thing happens in groups. We remember and hand on the meanings of one event that has made a difference to us. The same event has provided many deep meanings for the group, all of them true, but partial. These are traditions. Traditions are selective, too, whether they belong to an ethnic or a political or a religious group of human beings.

As individuals and as a people we remember the *meaning* of *events*, and that is what makes up *history*. One event, many meanings! One history, many memories! One Gospel, many ways of expressing it!

The Church, the people of God, receives the help of the Spirit to remember and preserve and make present again the meaning of the Lord Jesus, and not just some relic, or photograph, or museum monument. In four different Gospels the Church has recognized different meanings of the one Gospel that it proclaims. Its different communities remember one Lord, one faith, one baptism in locally different ways.

The Church preserves, ponders, develops, and presents the story of Jesus in each age. Development has occurred whenever the one universal Church, the "great Church," compares the memory of one group of her people with the memory of another community of her daughters and sons.[2] This happened in the early Church, and it happens now.[3]

While we are used to understanding this aspect of our tradition in the light of third and fourth century controversies about Jesus or about the Trinity, we have forgotten that it also happened earlier. Paul contrasted his understanding of the Gospel to Peter's and to that of other apostolic preachers. The author of 2 Peter (3:15) corrected those who misunderstood Paul's letters. Matthew and Luke developed the understanding of Mary in Mark's Gospel. They also remembered many sayings of the Lord which Mark did not include. Yet Luke's proclamation of Mary's role in the sacred history of Jesus differs from Matthew's. So it should not really surprise us that the Gospel of John develops the memories of other communities and presents the universal Church—which accepted it—with a different expression of the sacred history of the Lord which includes a development of the memory of Mary.

The story of Jesus as John portrays it is colored by a "high Christology."[4] He and his community remember above all the divinity of Jesus. This memory is put together in a composition which is rich in symbols and literary techniques. In this way the community proclaims the divine Jesus, Word and eternal Son of the Father, model and meaning of creation, light of the world, king of truth, manifestation in flesh of the glory of God. This faith is expressed in symbols of light and darkness, the heavens above and the earth below, flesh and spirit, error and truth, life and death, power and weakness, water and thirst, bread and hunger, wine and blood.

John's community is quite aware that this kind of symbolism is hard to understand. They even *say* that it takes growth in faith to pass from literal and superficial meanings of symbols to their deep and true meaning. They are aware of the other traditions in the Church at large, and they want to show that underneath it all, deeper than all apostleship, deeper than discipleship and the cross and all service, is *love*. They insist on this. The main figure of belief for them is the "beloved disciple." They proclaim the Gospel as a creation story, the religious way of speaking of the meaning of the whole world from its absolute origin in God. They picture Jesus, the royal king, before whom soldiers fall back because he lays down his own life and is not overcome by "the world," as washing the feet of his disciples to show what his authority means. They have Jesus tell Peter about loving the Lord before he can feed the sheep as a keeper of the keys. They remember Jesus on the cross as the risen and glorified lamb of God who gives everything away to his disciples out of love.[5]

The composer of the Gospel used archetypal figures without names to get this meaning across. He used an intricate arrangement of signs with deeper meanings, of sacred times, and of the relationship of origins to ends.[6] Titles encapsulate meanings. Flesh manifests the shining glory of God. Humanity reveals divinity.

That method of composition is very different from what we saw in the Synoptic Gospels. It gives us a memory our Church treasures. It is an important part of our *sacred history* which we can remember, and in which we can participate by coming to *know* Jesus. It includes Mary.

John's Gospel helps us to *know about* Mary, her meaning, so that we can come to *know* her or take her "into our own" (19:27). It does this through the way it is put together. So we have to start with how it is composed.

The Gospel relates origins to end. It begins with the same words as the Book of Genesis, known to John's community. In olden days books were known by their first words, not by titles as in our time. These first words of the old and the new Genesis—for the Gospel is being presented as a new Book of Genesis—are "In the beginning," the ritual formula for a creation account in almost every religion.[7] John looks backward to move forward, as we saw the Synoptic Gospel composers do. He moves backward from the death/resurrection of Jesus to the public life and back, not to the infancy of Jesus, but to the beginning of creation. He means to show by this technique who Jesus is and what he meant. Jesus brings the truth of creation about—a new creation, but new only in the sense that it was always planned and the Jewish people, except for Jesus' disciples, never recognized it.

The story of Jesus' public ministry is related to the story of his death/resurrection. Origins and end come together again.[8] Jesus' cross/glorification began in his public ministry, through signs which pointed to "the hour" of his glory on the cross. Everything from chapter 2 to chapter 13 points to the "hour," the last "Passover." Chapter 1 points to the whole rest of the Gospel. Chapter 13 to the end explains the preface and the public ministry. This is all done through "signs" or portrayals of Jesus which can only be explained by what happens later. While this technique of composition sounds very complicated, it isn't. The reader or hearer of the Gospel gets the message pretty clearly, at least with a little explanation. The scholar who studies the technique in order to recapture what John's own community got out of it has a harder time to explain *how* the author did what comes across so much more easily to the reader. The scholar can help explain the more intricate techniques and symbols, too, which may escape the reader or hearer in our own day.[9] It is like what happens in reading or studying poetry.

Let us use as an example of John's composition and portrayal of meaning in the parts of his Gospel which concern Mary. Mary is a part of John's memory of Jesus in both his public life and in his "hour" of death and glorification. In fact, she is singled out in a particular episode in each part of the Gospel. And if she is singled out, it must be for a special reason—which we shall see.

After the magnificent "creation hymn" of the prologue to the Gospel, John begins to tell us of "signs" done by Jesus, and explained by Jesus at the time he did them or during his "hour." He does this in a series of "signs" by enumerating days. All of these "signs" led to the final one, the day of the cross and glorification. The first sign that Jesus did, on the "third day," was at Cana in Galilee.[10] "The mother of Jesus was there." No name—just one of the three titles given to Mary by John.[11]

What was the sign that Jesus gave, and to whom? It takes place at a wedding to which the mother of Jesus, Jesus, and his disciples are invited. The bridegroom is not named. The bride isn't mentioned. The mother of Jesus notices that the wine is running out. She tells Jesus about it. He says to her, "Woman, what is that to me and to you? My hour has not yet come." Mary says to the servants, "Do whatever he tells you." Jesus tells the servants to take the ritual water jars, which were very large, and to fill them with water. Then Jesus tells them to take the water, made wine, to the person directing the feast, who tastes the wine. He doesn't know where it came from, but the servants do. The director tells the bridegroom that this is an unusual procedure since the best wine is usually served first but in this case the best wine was saved till this moment.

There is no mention of the bridegroom's reaction. The story goes on to tell that the disciples of Jesus believed in him because of this sign which revealed his glory.

Now that is a strange ending. Like an "in" joke, it demands some kind of inside knowledge to know how the ending follows from the strange story. What kind of memory of Jesus is this? How was it so important that it was taken up by the writer of the Gospel and made into the very first "sign"? And why is Mary part of the story, with that strange dialogue?

I suppose those who have heard the story many times just presume that Jesus worked an astounding miracle, and that made the disciples believe in him. But this "sign" tells us much more than that.

Let us look at the story more closely. As the first "sign" of Jesus' public ministry after the prologue, it is supposed to point to the following part of the Gospel where Jesus is glorified in his death and resurrection. Second, we know that the story says that only his disciples saw this connection or manifestation of glory, and believed. Third, there are some important details in the story that make up the very substance of the sign that teaches the disciples about Jesus' glory.

To get more out of the details, and so to understand the story better, let us think of how some of us get more out of a story when we pay attention to details. Let us say we are at a Thanksgiving Day liturgy in an American parish, and we have brought along a friend from a foreign country. One of the participants in the liturgy gets up and tells a story about what Thanksgiving Day means to her belief. She says that she has found God in the gifts she received from poor people, just as the pilgrims found God's blessings in the turkeys given to them by the Indian people. And she thanks God. After she sits down, our foreign friend asks what turkeys and pilgrims mean. Only upon explanation of the details from someone familiar with where the details come from can there be understanding.

The details in the Cana story are many. There's the third day theme, the wedding, the lack of attention to the bride and groom, the water jars, the fact that Mary is called only the "mother of Jesus" and "woman" but never "Mary," the servants who knew where the water/wine came from, the director, and even more. What did these details mean to the people in John's community?

First of all, they are biblical. John's people were familiar with the feasts and Scriptures of the Jews.[12] Very familiar! And they were familiar with Cana and the geography of Judea.[13] And they must have been familiar with the role of the mother of Jesus in relation to the disciples' belief in Jesus' glory.[14]

Second, the community of John picked up the difference between new and old, Jew and Christian, the old creation and the new creation, right away. They knew that the whole Gospel was called by its first words, "In the beginning," just as Genesis, the creation and introduction to the law of the Jews, was called by the same first words, "In the beginning." So they knew that the Cana story meant something about the new creation happening "now" at Cana, even though it pointed to the cross and glorification of Jesus and the full faith that started the community of the new creation later in the Gospel.

Third, they were familiar with what "signs" meant. They knew that Jesus taught through signs, so that people moved from seeing Jesus as a wonder worker alone, to seeing him as the promised Messiah and prophet, until they finally saw him, through his signs, as the very divine source of all creation and its true meaning.

Therefore, if we look at the details, we see that the great biblical messianic banquet, an Old Testament familiar theme, is taking place. There will be a new wine and a new gift of the spirit which will make the believers drunk with joy.[15] The old temple rituals will fall away before the new temple, Jesus.[16] The officials and non-believing Jews will not understand. Only servants of the banquet will know where the wine comes from as the final "hour" of the Lord begins.[17] Although Jesus says that his hour has not yet come, his signs start the process of glorification on the cross and faith-participation by his disciples in that process.[18]

And what about Mary? She is presented to an understanding community as *the* special mother, like the Genesis woman, Eve, and like all women who believe in Jesus, and like the Church of birth-giving community.[19] She is the one whose role it was and is, in memory and present understanding, to start the process, to notice the lack of wine and the Spirit, to talk to the servants but not to the officials, to understand what Jesus is doing and will do, and to represent that motto of the Christian, "Do whatever he tells you."[20]

She is remembered as the mother of Jesus who is also the woman of the new creation. No little tribute that! But this memory points to its further explanation in the second episode, at the foot of the cross.

The story of the wedding which took place in Galilee points to the "hour" of Jesus in Jerusalem. It mentions this "hour" as not yet arrived, but anticipated for the faithful. The story has a follow-up immediately in the Gospel. It says that Jesus went to Capernaum to spend a few days with his mother, his brothers, and his disciples. Those "brothers" were not part of the wedding feast. They did not see "greater signs" on "the third day," the day of the resurrection and the new creation, the way disciples like Nathanael did. Just before the wedding story Jesus said to Nathanael that he would see greater signs. The disciples did, at the wedding feast of the Messiah. They began to see his glory—but not the "brothers" of the Lord. They, in fact, are called "unbelievers" (7:5). They will not be part of the hour of death and glory.

Recall that Mark's memory was that Mary and the brothers of the Lord were considered together as misunderstanding Jesus' meaning. Matthew softens that picture of Mary, but still considers the mother and relatives of Jesus together as having no blood rights to the new order. Luke portrays the memory that Mary was the faithful virgin, disciple of the Father, open to the kingdom. But he retains the memory of Mark, too, that Mary and the relatives of Jesus are remembered together. They all agree that the new family of God comes only through faith. This is the eschatological family, the people of God in the final times, related by a community of faith and worship.[21]

John adds a twist to this traditional memory of Mary and the relatives. Since the Gospel was written at a time when James, the "brother" of the Lord, was known as a famous disciple, John's twist has added emphasis. He leaves the brothers of the Lord out altogether. They are unbelievers. He separates them from the memory of Mary. They will have no part in the "hour," but she will.[22]

In the next and final part of the Gospel the meaning of Jesus' "hour" is proclaimed. As R.H. Fuller describes the "hour," "everything prior to it is provisional." There the signs of Jesus find their fulfillment. There the water of Jewish ritual is replaced by the new wine of Jesus' blood. The *hour* is when he saves us from death and blindness and being crippled. There, at the passion and death and resurrection in one narrative of the royal crucifixion and glorification of Jesus, the revelation of all Jesus' discourses becomes reality. It is "the crucified-glorified One who is the true bread from heaven, the light of the world, the door of the sheep, the Good Shepherd, the resurrection and the life, the way, the truth and the life, and the true vine."[23]

We saw that the story of the wedding banquet at Cana pointed to the new creation and new convenant where servants recognize the source of the new wine of the Spirit. Mary was not rebuffed by Jesus in their dialogue. She turned to the servants and told them Jesus would "do" something about the condition of the Spirit-less rituals of the Jewish covenant. She knew that Jesus would fulfill the promises and that good Jewish servants of the Lord would listen to him. She is very connected with that "hour."

In chapter 19 we see just how connected Mary was with the hour of Jesus in the sacred memory of the Johannine Christian community. In the other Gospels the disciples flee from the cross. A few women stand at a distance along with some of Jesus' acquaintances. Mary does not. But in John's Gospel some of the women stand at the very foot of the cross. There is a reason for this depiction of Mary.[24]

The cross is the place and time of the final revelation and glorification of Jesus in the Johannine memory.[25] It is the sacred *hour* of his death, burial, resurrection, and gift of the Spirit. By the next morning, the day after the sabbath of the Jews, Jesus' resurrection becomes known. The composer of the Gospel adds stories of later appearances of the risen Lord only to explain the meaning of the *hour*. The scene at the cross is the way that the Gospel describes the birth of the Church.[26] This scene is the "climax," the fulfillment of all the signs Jesus did. It is also the fulfillment of the old creation and the old covenant. And Mary has a special role in the scene.

It is important to see how the writer relates origins and end in this scene through symbols and characters he has used before to point to this event. If we examine the symbols and characters it will become clearer how origins and end are related.[27]

First the symbols. The most interesting for us, but not the only symbols in this scenario, are water, wine, banquet, servants, and authority.

Water has been a symbol throughout the Gospel. In 1:19–34 John the Baptist, prophet of the old covenant who baptizes with water, proclaims Jesus to be the servant or lamb of God who baptizes with water and the Holy Spirit. At Cana the waters of the Jewish covenant are turned into the wine of the Holy Spirit at the messianic banquet (2:1–11). Jesus tells Nicodemus that baptism in water and the Holy Spirit is a rebirth from above, and refers to his "hour" of death and exaltation (3:3–15). John the Baptist describes Jesus' baptism with water and the Spirit in 3:22–36. He refers to Jesus as the "bridegroom" who gives the Spirit and eternal life.

In chapter four the water symbolism grows. Jesus speaks to the

Samaritan woman at Jacob's well. He promises her living water of eternal life. He tells her that the "hour" is coming when a new worship in Spirit and truth will replace the covenant as both Jews and Samaritans understood it. Those who truly believe ("heard" for themselves) proclaim him "Savior of the world." The Gospel then says that Jesus returned to Cana, "where he made the water wine," and cures the official's son at Capernaum. This official came looking for a sign, but believed in Jesus' words, and at that "hour" he received life.

In chapter five at a pool of water Jesus cures a sick man on the sabbath. The leaders of the Jews object to this since it was the sabbath of their law. Jesus says that he can give life to whomever he wills and that he fulfills the Scriptures and the law of Moses. He refers to the testimony of John the Baptist. There is a baptismal context to the pool in the story.

Chapter six turns to the symbol of *bread,* but uses the same significance that the Gospel gave to *water.* Jesus is the bread of life, greater than the manna of the old covenant. To eat his flesh gives eternal life. The same is true of his blood. To drink his blood gives eternal life. Then he speaks of his death and ascension back to the Father, and of the Spirit who gives life.

Chapter seven returns to the symbol of water. First Jesus says that he fulfills the sabbath and the law of Moses. Then he says, "If anyone thirsts let him come to me and drink." The Gospel explains this as reference to the Spirit to be given at his glorification. The background of the "living water" is the wisdom and prophetic literature of the Hebrew Scriptures.

In chapter twelve Mary, sister of Lazarus, washes Jesus' feet with precious ointment and wipes them with her hair. Jesus refers to his burial. Then in chapter thirteen, when Jesus knew that his "hour" had started, Jesus washes and dries the feet of his disciples. Jesus explains that they will only understand this later (15:3), for not only does he wash their feet but he bathes them clean of sin. He tells them that they must follow his example and wash one another's feet as servants, since they are not greater than their master who is a "servant" in the Gospel.

This example of *service* is given at the Passover *banquet* which is the beginning of Jesus' "hour." This is the messianic banquet which fulfills the hope and promises of the old covenant. This is the further enactment of the wedding banquet of Cana. The old is being replaced by being fulfilled. The ritual *waters* of the old dispensation are replaced with the new water of eternal life to come from Jesus' side, which gives the Spirit. The waters of the Jews of old have become the *wine* that gives the Spirit. This was promised in the prophets. Now it is being fulfilled. There is no story of the institution of the Eucharist in the memory of this community in the precise formula remembered by Paul or the Synoptic Gospels. The wine of this banquet, the wine of the Spirit and the new law, is the *blood* of Christ spoken of in chapter six—the blood which gives life has to be drunk. This "good wine" is saved until last, as the Cana story said. At the last this blood/wine is the water that issues from the side of Christ, the water that accompanies the gift of the *Spirit*.[28] And just as the *servants* at Cana knew where the new wine came from, so the disciples are told by the Lord about how to be *servants* (12:26; 13:16; 15:12–17; 15:20–21). Servants must follow the new commandment of love above all. That is what authority means. It is as servant, lamb of God, that Jesus gives the Spirit whom he speaks of at the banquet (14:16; 14:26; 15:26; 16:7).[29]

All of the symbols come together in the "hour." At the climax, the scene at the cross, the symbols are brought to bear on two characters: the mother of Jesus and the beloved disciple. There has been a tremendous build-up of narratives and discourses to this point. It will all focus on these two participants in Jesus' deathly triumph.

None of the other Gospels mentions these two characters at the foot of the cross. There is a reason for their being there in John's Gospel. The reason is not pedestrian. This is a strongly symbolic memory of the birth of the Church and the meaning of Christian life. To say that what happens between Jesus and these two unnamed archetypal figures is only that Jesus wanted someone to take care of his mother would be to destroy the dramatic build-up and to start talking "biography" in our modern way of looking at history. The very garments Jesus was wearing are imbued with deep symbolism. Jesus did not leave them to poor people. Just before he speaks to the two characters his garments are described. They are a symbol of undivided unity among Jesus' followers—a symbol which fulfills the Scriptures. The statement that the beloved disciple took Jesus' mother "into his own life" is symbolic and laden with deep meaning, too. Jesus' last will and testament is not concerned with natural affairs.[30]

Jesus speaks to his mother first. Then he speaks to the "beloved disciple." His mother is more important in the dialogue from the start. Jesus does not call her by name but by the Genesis title used in Cana: "woman." He reveals, "behold," that the beloved disciple is to be her son. Jesus is explaining something about Cana. At Cana Jesus anticipated the "hour" of the new creation and the new covenant. He gave Mary a title and function which can only be understood in the light of the old creation in Genesis and the old covenant of Moses, the prophets, and the wisdom writings. The waters of the Jewish rituals have been changed into the waters of eternal life given by the Spirit. This title "woman" belonged to the mother of all the living in the old creation, and to Israel the mother of God's chosen children in the old covenant. It belonged to Israel in synonymous ways: bride, mother, daughter, all derived necessarily from her relationship to God as mother of those who lived in the covenant. Mary's function is to be "mother of the beloved disciple," another title bestowed in this moment of judgment on Mary through the words spoken by Jesus to the beloved disciple. Her firstborn in the new creation and new covenant, the eschatological family, is the beloved disciple.[31]

Jesus then speaks to the beloved disciple. This unnamed person receives a new title, too: "son of the mother who is woman in the new creation and new covenant." His first title pointed out his function in the community: the archetypal example of loving service. He had authority in the community of the new family because, like the servants at Cana, he knew where the "good wine" came from. He followed the words of the Woman at Cana: "Do whatever He tells you." He exemplified love and what it meant to be a servant, disciple, and friend of the Lord in the way Jesus explained at the messianic banquet of the last Passover.

The words of Jesus to the beloved disciple are too symbolic to be taken as a way Jesus could take care of his mother in an earthly sense. The scene makes them much more meaningful. The beloved disciple "took her into his own life." He saw Mary with the eyes of faith and accepted her as his mother in his rebirth from above. As soon as he does this, Jesus says "I thirst" to show his desire to drink the bitter wine of death and fulfill the mission of the Father from the beginning of time. Then he knew that "all was fulfilled" and "gave over his Spirit." The soldiers pierce his side and "blood and water" come out (see 7:38). There is a new creation, and a new covenant ritual starts. His glory was accomplished. He returned to the Father. They put his body in a grave, but would not find him there. He had risen in his eternal glory.

These titles of the mother of Jesus and of the beloved disciple must have been understandable to the community as part of their sacred memory. They were important figures in their proclamation of faith. They give the beloved disciple a special right to authority in the community. He exemplifies not only that the commandment of love comes first for all leaders, even Peter (20:4–10; 21:15–18), but also that his eyewitness testimony is guaranteed by his being "son of the woman." Mary is the "maternal rememberer" whose special relationship to the beloved disciple and to all whom he represents guarantees the truth of their belief. His testimony is "true" because she guarantees that those who love and serve are those who "do whatever the Lord tells them."

In all of this the Gospel has been speaking about the relationship between origins and ends. Through the symbols and characters of the narratives and discourses, the community remembers the absolute origin and final goal of the world. The origin of Jesus as the enfleshment of the eternal Word of God is related to his end: death, resurrection, gift of the Spirit, and return to his Father. The beginning of Jesus' public life of "signs" is related to his "hour." The use of one symbol starts in one story and ends up in another which often refers back to the first one. In each case the Word-in-flesh is at the center.[32]

Mary and the beloved disciples are not central to the Johannine community's sacred memory. The Lord is. But they have an essential role to play as the community looks backward to understand itself and to live as Christians. Their roles come from their titles. The beloved disciple is the exemplar of loving service of the Lord. As "son of the woman" he is the guarantee of the authenticity of the memory handed on. Mary is the "mother of Jesus," "the woman," and "mother of the beloved disciple." As "mother of Jesus" she guarantees the validity of the humanity of the Word of God. But she is not depicted further for her natural blood maternal relationship to Jesus. It is the eschatological family who are the true children of God, those who have been reborn "from above" (1:13). As "woman" Mary is remembered as the example of all women in a new creation, the woman of a new Genesis, the true Jewish mother-Israel who recognizes the need of the Spirit's new wine and indicates to those who are servants of God, especially Jews, how to take part in the messianic banquet. As "mother of the beloved disciple" the community remembered her as the woman they must take into their own lives as the beloved disciple did—that is, she symbolizes the Church who gives the Spirit and guarantees the memory of Jesus. By recognizing the Church as the community of brotherly and sisterly love, Mary becomes known as mother to every brother and sister of the Lord.

This sacred group memory of the Johannine community adds to the memory of the other Gospels. Her holiness and maternity are part of a "high Christological memory." She is *archetypal* mother and model and woman in the new creation.

REFERENCES

1. On this diversity within unity see R.E. Brown, *The Churches the Apostles Left Behind* (New York: Paulist Press, 1984), pp. 19–31 and 146 ff; Y. Congar, O.P., *Diversity and Communion*, translated by J. Bowden (Mystic: Twenty-Third Publications, 1984), pp. 12–13; R.E. Brown, *Biblical Exegesis and Church Doctrine* (New York: Paulist Press, 1985), pp. 123–134.

2. R.E. Brown uses the phrase "the great Church" and explains it in *The Epistles of John* (New York: Doubleday and Co., 1982), Anchor Bible, Vol. 30, p. 103, note 2.

3. See R.E. Brown, *The Churches the Apostles Left Behind*, pp. 146–150; T. Jimenez-Urresti, "The Ontology of Communion and Collegial Structures in the Church," in *Pastoral Reform in Church Government*, Concilium 8 (New York: Paulist Press, 1965), p. 13; David Tracy, "Ethnic Pluralism and Systematic Theolgy: Reflections," in *Ethnicity*, ed. by A. Greeley and G. Baum, Concilium, 101 (New York: Seabury Press, 1977), pp. 91–99.

4. On "high Christology" see J. Fitzmeyer, S.J., *A Christological Catechism* (New York: Paulist Press, 1982), p. 65.

5. The first words of the Gospel and the constant references to "beginning" and to the Jewish creation stories shape the message of the Gospel. See R.E. Brown, *The Gospel According to John [I–XII]* (New York: Doubleday and Co., 1966), Anchor Bible, Vol. 29, pp. 4, 139, 178; A. Feuillet, *Johannine Studies*, translated by T.E. Crane (New York: Alba House, 1964), pp. 20, 30, 260–270; J. Marsh, "John: A Very Different Gospel?" in *A Companion to John*, edited by M. Taylor, S.J. (New York: Alba House, 1977), p. 10.

6. See J. Grassi, "The Role of Jesus' Mother in John's Gospel: A Re-Appraisal," *Catholic Biblical Quarterly*, 48/1986, pp. 67–80; P.F. Ellis, *The Genius of John* (Collegeville: Liturgical Press, 1985), pp. 13ff; J. Staley, "The Structure of John's Prologue: Its Implications for the Gospel Narrative Structure," *Catholic Biblical Quarterly*, 48/1986, pp. 241–264.

7. On the formula "In the beginning" see R. Pettazzoni, *Essays on the History of Religions*, translated by H.J. Rose (Leiden: E.J. Brill, 1967), pp. 21, 28, 36; M. Eliade, *Myth and Reality*, translated by W.R. Trask (New York: Harper and Row, 1963), pp. 36–38; T.W. Manson, "The Johannine Jesus as Logos," in *A Companion to John*, ed. Taylor, *cited above*, p. 40; B. De Pinto, "John's Jesus: Biblical Wisdom and the Word Embodied," *ibid.*, pp. 59–60.

8. There are two senses in which origins and end come together. There is the literary structure of chiastic forms—see Staley's *cited article*, pp. 251, 264 or Grassi's *article already cited*, p. 69 for examples—and the symbolic structure of thought upon which this form is based. This structure of symbolic thought is especially evident in creation accounts in most religions. See G. van der Leeuw, "Primordial Time and Final Time," Papers from Eranos Yearbooks, No. 3, *Man and Time*, edited by J. Campbell (New York: Pantheon Books, 1957), especially pp. 325ff. The end of all the creation (of the world) in this sense is, for John, the resurrection of Jesus and participation in it by true disciples.

9. See S.M. Schneiders, I.H.M., "From Exegesis to Hermeneutics: The Problem of the Contemporary Meaning of Scripture," *Horizons* 8/1981, pp. 23–39; R.A. Culpepper, *Anatomy of the Fourth Gospel* (Philadelphia: Fortress Press, 1983), pp. 211ff on "the implied reader."

10. On the significance of "the third day" at Cana see I. de la Potterie, "Mary and the Mystery of Cana," *Theology Digest*, 29/1981, pp. 40–42; A. Feuillet, *Johannine Studies*, p. 34, n. 35; J. Huckle and P. Visokay, *The Gospel According to John*, Vol. 1 (New York: Crossroad, 1981), pp. 22–26.

11. Titles are the beginnings of theology in a religion. In ancient religions the listing of the titles of a God were praises, summations of the various meanings of the divine, and reflective comparisons of attributes and meanings. This persists in almost every religion in titles, doxologies, and litanies. The titles of Jesus are very important for the study of Christology and the history of doxologies is important for the study of Christian tradition. See G. Wainwright, *Doxology* (New York: Oxford University Press, 1984), pp. 46ff, 157ff.

12. See Brown, *The Gospel According to John (I–XII), cited above*, p. lx.

13. See Brown, *ibid.*, pp. xliiff; R.A. Culpepper, *book cited above*, pp. 216ff.

14. I find it strange that Culpepper does not list the mother of Jesus among the characters the audience would recognize. There must be some kind of historical basis to John's ever widening circle of symbolism: mother of Jesus, mother and brothers, woman, mother of the beloved disciple. A purely symbolic interpretation of the woman as only a metaphor for the good synagogue or for the new Church-mother avoids the historical basis in the text. Historical basis does not demand a fundamentalist or literal or naive expectation of pictorial details. In fact no history gives that as we have seen. But the identification of characters and perhaps—we cannot know for sure—certain events such as a wedding at Cana or the identification of people at the foot of the cross provide the "fact" part of the "fact with

meaning," while the "meaning" part of such history allows developed symbolism. See R.A. Fuller, "The Passion, Death and Resurrection of Jesus According to St. John," in *The Passion, Death and Resurrection of the Lord* (Mundelein: Chicago Studies, 1985), p. 56; F.J. Moloney, S.D.B., *Woman: First Among the Faithful, cited above*, pp. 101–102. See notes 20 and 27 below.

15. See A. Feuillet, *Johannine Studies*, cited above, pp. 31ff and 76ff.

16. See Brown, *The Gospel According to John [I–XII]*, p. 104.

17. See Grassi, *article cited*, pp. 76, 78.

18. See Fuller, *article cited*, p. 52.

19. See P.F. Ellis, *book cited above*, pp. 271–272; F.J. Moloney, *book cited*, p. 103.

20. While these words which the evangelist puts into Mary's mouth may be reminders of the Hebrew creeds of covenant renewal, we should be cautious about making out of these words only a theological presentation, as A. Feuillet (*work cited*, p. 37) cautions about the interpretation of Charlier for the words "they have no wine." If the role of Mary here is fairly well estimated to be the "maternal rememberer," the judgment of Grassi (*art. cited*, p. 78, n. 24), her words would justify John's peculiar emphasis on "authority as loving service" in the new creation (15:14ff).

21. See *Mary in the New Testament, cited above*, p. 218.

22. See *Mary in the New Testament*, pp. 200, 213.

23. See Fuller, *article cited*, p. 52; W.D. Davies, "The Johannine 'Signs' of Jesus," in *A Companion to John, cited above*, pp. 112–115.

24. See *Mary in the New Testament*, pp. 206–210.

25. See Grassi, *article cited*, p. 69.

26. See P.F. Ellis, *book cited above*, pp. 274–312.

27. The symbolism of titles is evident. That is not to say that there is no historicity involved. See *Mary in the New Testament*, p. 209. John, as a prophet, is "revealing the significance of events," as P.S. Minear puts it in *John—The Martyr's Gospel* (New York: Pilgrim Press, 1984), p. 12. There is *hermeneutic* present in the Gospel as we have it. The Gospel explains the deep symbolic truth of the event. See F. Mussner, *The Historical Jesus in the Gospel of John*, translated by W.J. O'Hara (New York: Herder and Herder, 1967). In fact John is showing the faith-ground of his community by claiming a guarantee of his testimony and presentation through the "substitution" of the beloved disciple for Jesus, a "brother of the Lord" in the new creation or "eschatological family" or "Church," whose testimony is related to Mary as "maternal rememberer" or archetypal guarantee of eyewitness testimony. All of these claims have to do with the meaning of the Gospel to John's community at that time. To preclude empirical basis for the symbolism of archetypal figures would be to err on one side, as to preclude symbolic interpretation would err on the other side. See R. Needham, *Primordial Characters* (Charlottesville: University Press of Virginia, 1978), pp. 27–31. See note 8 above on "origins and end."

28. See Jn 10:17–18; 18:6,37. The "spirit" in 19:30 should be understood in the context of John's composition which relates the "spirit" to creation and birth. See 1:13,33; 3:5; 4:4; 6:54–56; 7:37–38; 19:34. The following scenes are dramatic explanations of the meaning of the glorification of the Lord: ascension, reception of the Spirit, transcendence of Jesus in the new creation. If we saw the gift of the Spirit at the cross as prolepsis only, a way of saying what would happen later in 20:22, the element of "time" would become very non-symbolic, very conceptual and literal. But just as "hour" means more than "a sixty minute time span" other instances of time are bound by the meaning of the writer in the composition as a whole. "Hour" and "Passover" and "first day" say much more than they would seem to say at first glance. The "handing over" of his Spirit by the Word-made-flesh at the moment of his "hour" which fulfills

the plan of all creation from the beginning places Mary in connection with the Spirit. She and the disciple are there when the Spirit is given. The disciple believes when he gets to the empty tomb. So also she who is Jesus' mother in the flesh has a role of faith to play. She "sees," too, or is "glorified" in John's sense of that word. She understands her place (signified at Cana) by the gift of the Spirit. Her place is her relationship to the beloved disciple and his testimony. See R.A. Culpepper, *work cited*, pp. 134, 165, 195, 226; J. Grassi, *article cited*, pp. 74–77.

29. For more information on the symbolism of water in John, see A. Feuillet, *work cited*, pp. 76–82, and R.E. Brown, "The Qumran Scrolls and John," in *A Companion to John*, *cited above*, pp. 86ff.

30. For more information on "the beloved disciple," see Pheme Perkins, "Johannine Literature: From Text to Community," in *The Biblical Heritage in Modern Catholic Scholarship*, ed. by J.J. Collins and J.D. Crossan (Wilmington: M. Glazier, 1986), pp. 184–211. On the meaning of "into his own" see R.E. Brown, *The Gospel According to John [XIII–XXI]* (New York: Doubleday and Co., 1970), p. 907; J. Grassi, *article cited*, p. 73.

31. The analysis of symbolism shows us that a symbol, unlike a concept, is polyvalent. Symbols have many meanings at once. Concepts are monovalent, expressions of one sole meaning which is abstracted from the symbol's many meanings. This helps us to appreciate the *meaning* of John's memory of Mary. She has to have three titles to express the variety and depth of her significance for the community. And there are presumed meanings underneath these three. Mary is a feminine person, image of God (Gen 1:27). She is a Jewish woman, from Galilee, and a mother. She becomes archetypal of each for John's community through her three titles. She represents the Jewish "woman" who bridges old and new creation, covenant, community, and ritual. Her Jewishness in John is not noticed enough. Sometimes it is taken apart from the other meanings. See P. Minear, *work cited*, p. 150 (against anti-semitism); Jane

Kopas, "Jesus and Women: John's Gospel," *Theology Today*, 41/2, July 1984, pp. 202–205.

32. The notion of *center* is used by D. Senior, "God's Creative Word at Work in Our Midst," in *The Sacraments: God's Love and Mercy Actualized*, ed. by F. Eigo (Villanova University Press, 1979), pp. 1–28.

5

THE DEVELOPMENT OF THE MEMORY OF MARY IN THE EARLY CHURCH

S ome people picture King Henry VIII speaking English the way it is spoken in London today. Some people think that Julius Caesar went home to take a shower after work the way a person would today in Chicago. Some people think that Marian devotions existed in the early Christian communities the way they existed in our Catholic churches in the 1950's. History didn't happen that way. People have to have the chance to learn this.

The teachings and devotions of the Church developed out of the New Testament into compatible but different memories. It took some time for what we call "organization" and "liturgy" to develop. Our Church is a living community, developing its understanding with the help of the Holy Spirit. Our tradition is an historic one, based on the Lord and the Gospel memories preserved by the Church. But that does not mean that the early Church was a smaller and more pacific version of the present Church. The early days were very different from today in culture, in what people had as "experience" under their belts, in social settings, and in expressions of what they understood.

Marian theology and devotions as *we speak* of them did not exist in the earliest Church after the writing of the New Testament. But the memories that were sacred to the Church of the New Testament were there. And there was a development—often stormy. People should have a chance to learn this, too.

It is intriguing to try to discover the earliest developments in the Church's sacred memory not only of Mary, but of the story of the Lord in which her memory was enshrined. If we take care we can discover, like Howard Carter at King Tut's tomb, "wonderful things." If we do not take care all sorts of bad conclusions will be made.

Bad conclusions are being made today. The story of the origins of Marian devotions and doctrine makes good press today. It is not uncommon to come across books on the history of Christianity or on Marian "cult" which are the "latest" study on how goddess worship started among Christians after 431, when the Council of Ephesus declared that Mary was "Theotokos" or "Godbearer."[1]

The "bad conclusion" being made is that nothing happened in the Church before 431 which could have been the link between the New Testament memories of Mary and what later became the kind of Marian teaching and devotion of the Catholic Church in the twentieth century.

Someone might think: "Well, either it was there or it wasn't; these people couldn't get away with saying it all began in 431 if they are writing scholarly works and it was either there or it wasn't before 431." But history isn't that easy to understand.

The simplest historical statement actually includes much complexity. The historian Trevelyan once said that since her time all later history depended on the shape of Cleopatra's nose. That was a strange but simple statement. However, in reality it is very complex—or what it means is complex. It can only be understood if someone knows who Marc Antony was, whom he was fighting, why he was doing that, and why this Greek lady in Egypt entered his life, and what happened in their relationship, and how this shaped the development of the West. It also includes the idea that we don't know what the shape of her nose was, nor Marc's private likings.

To investigate what happened to the memory of Mary in the story of Jesus handed on in the Church communities after 100 A.D. includes all kinds of details, some of which we can never uncover, and all of which belong to a time and place far away and long ago. We can learn enough, if we take care, to understand some of what happened. And that will be enough to avoid bad conclusions either that Marian memories became important to the Christian people only after 431 or that you would find the same Marian teachings and prayers in the earliest days that you had in 1950.

As we mentioned in Chapter Four, "events" are "remembered happenings," and they are "remembered" because they "mean so much." This is our insight in historical studies today. We know that to get even a glimpse of what occurred in the past we have to find out how people in a certain time long gone expressed what was "meaningful" to them, how the social situation—insofar as we can know that—influenced their "expressions of meaning," and how we have to translate what they "meant" into how we "say what *we* mean" in our social contexts. We need much study and little prejudice. We have to be adept in the discipline of "interpretation" (*hermeneutics*) of texts, of different methods of arriving at "meaning" in history and social sciences, and in theology or psychology or any one particular area of "study" we use. It takes much study and complexity to arrive at a simple glimpse.

One good way to catch our glimpse of the memory of the unfolding and developing Church of the Lord insofar as it includes the memory and role of Mary is to start before 431 and move backward. Then we will see that 431 isn't the absolute start some scholars make it out to be, and we can study what had developed by that time to see if we can trace its roots. Then we will find, I think, "wonderful things" even if they are not the same as what we are used to today. This will also give us the roots for the growing picture that develops over the centuries, through good times and bad exaggerations, making contemporary memories of Mary possible.

We will start with St. Athanasius of Alexandria, who was a fiery sort of man and very alive—as were all leaders, men and women, at the time—from 295 to 373 A.D. He was an intellectual, a bishop, and a controversialist. His teachings influenced later thinkers and ecumenical councils.

The city of Alexandria was something like the Hong Kong of the Roman Empire—business, a large population, large bodies of ethnic groups who clung together, famous schools with an intellectual elite! Maybe it was more like New York for those days. Christians made their home there from the first century and had intellectual debates about new ideas (gnosticism). There were Christians from every social class. The bishops we know of were teachers and controversialists. Athanasius became bishop in 328. He had been the previous bishop's secretary and in that capacity attended the ecumenical Council of Nicea in 325. He made many enemies because of his opposition to the Arian Christians who denied that Jesus was true God and true man. He was exiled three times for his bold opposition to ideas that were politically "in" but which he said were contrary to the traditional faith. His writings became famous.[2]

Athanasius developed his theological reflections with constant reference to the practices and prayers of the ordinary people in his community. That is of special interest to us. The habitual prayers and liturgical practices of the people arose from earlier memories of the Lord, preserved and re-presented in formal and non-formal ways.[3]

Athanasius made some very important statements about the memory of Mary in the community's faith and prayer life. He referred to expressions of her meaning in the faith which were taken from earlier documents. He was very creative in relating past memories to present situations. He united in a new way the different expressions of Mary's role in the work of the Lord. He justified this by claiming that this was the meaning of past religious practices and theological statements. His theology of Mary in belief and prayer life can help us to glimpse in what way earlier communities of his Church, and other communities which were in contact with this important center, remembered Mary.

What Athanasius said about Mary came out of his controversy with a group called "Neo-Arians." This was just one of the violent controversies in which he engaged. Not that they were of his choosing. Bishops and emperors were competing and colluding for power. All kinds of variations of explanations of the teachings of the Council of Nicaea were being broadcast. Athanasius was a traditionalist.

The Neo-Arians denied that Jesus was fully human. They said that the Divine Word merely associated himself with a human body. Athanasius wrote that these "explanations" were worse than the heretical thoughts of the earlier Arians. He insisted that the Divine Logos became human by "being born of the Virgin Mary, the *Theotokos.*" He repeats the traditional explanation that Jesus' humanity was guaranteed by being "born of the Virgin Mary." He adds the title of Mary, "*Theotokos,*" to this. He justifies his addition. This is the title given to Mary in the public tradition of prayer among the orthodox Christian people of Alexandria. He insists that orthodoxy has to include traditional explanation and traditional cultic prayer.

This is how Athanasius expressed it: "If the Logos is of one essence with the body, the commemoration (*mneme*) and the office (*chreia*) of Mary are superfluous." He is saying that there was a liturgical remembrance of Mary, a *mneme*, which guaranteed the humanity of the incarnate Logos. And this cultic prayer remembered her role (*chreia*) in the economy of salvation in the past and in the present. Not only was Mary's motherhood important in the Church as a past event, a guarantee for belief in the humanity of Jesus, but her role is part of the ongoing working out of salvation by Christians in their life of prayer in the present. The present memory of her role is not superfluous![4]

Athanasius did something very important in the history of theology. His theology of Christ is united to his theology of the Church. He showed the importance of Mary in this theology. Since the sacred memory of Jesus which was handed on in the New Testament is for the present Church's faith and worship and ascetical life, he showed that the present day memory of Mary in the practice of the Church, liturgical and ascetical, was not only a guarantee of the humanity of Jesus the Lord in our faith, but a memory of her special function in the working out of the plan of God for all times. He describes this special function in two ways. Mary is "Theotokos." And Mary is the model of a holy Christian life.

He says that Mary is remembered in the cultic prayers of his community as "Theotokos." This title was not in the Gospels. Later it will be made official at the ecumenical Council of Ephesus (431). But he shows that it is orthodox, for it is the liturgical way of proclaiming belief in the humanity of Jesus. The "economy of salvation" is not speculative theology, separated from cult, but the unity of theology-liturgy in the life of faith. In such "theology" the title "Theotokos" is not only a theological statement of guarantee regarding Jesus' human nature, it is a title of Mary including devotion. The New Testament had made similar statements showing that Mary guaranteed Jesus' humanity. Jesus was "born of a woman, born under the law." Jesus was "born of the Virgin Mary." But this title "Theotokos" is added on in the worshiping community at Alexandria. It was used by Bishop Alexander in 325. It appears in the even older hymn, the "Sub Tuum Praesidium" which said "We fly to thy protection, O Holy *Theotokos*." This hymn probably arose in the Egyptian community, and may have been an adaptation of a pagan religious title of Isis as "mother of the god" to the people's usage of the New Testament. If so, it would have received new meaning as a title. But it would have shown, anyway, the tender devotion of the people to the woman who was remembered as the virgin mother of Jesus.

The fact that such devotion was included in the usage of this title by Athanasius, who claimed the liturgical usage as his source, is shown by what he says about Mary in his *Letter to the Virgins*. There he does what one historian of Christian theology has called "development by extrapolation." Athanasius says in his *Letter* that Mary is remembered by the Church not in the way the Old Testament prophets are remembered. Rather, she is remembered because she had a role in the work of Christ. What kind of a role? She was a human being only, but she was holy. In order to understand how she was holy, he "extrapolates" to his own day. It must have been similar to the way women were holy in his community. Or men. She must have been a model of asceticism. So he proposes Mary as the model for virgins who lived an ascetical life in his community.[5]

Athanasius' explanation of the humanity of Jesus and the human holiness of Mary included another interesting theological development. He was attempting to explain how the memory of Mary was preserved in the memory of Jesus, and how Mary was special in the memory of Jesus and its present meaning for Christians. His opponents, the Arians, had spoken of Jesus as a "perfect creature." He said that that was not an orthodox language in which to present the New Testament memory of Jesus. Jesus, said Athanasius, could not be called a "creature." The only human who could claim our reverence by being called a "perfect creature" would be Mary. She is a creature. She is "our sister" who became a childless widow at the foot of the cross. She had to progress from doubt to faith and grow in holiness. But God dwelled in her in such a way that she became the model of God's indwelling in his creatures. As the "mother of God" who provided the Divine Logos with true human nature, she was also the mother who was a model of holiness. The memory of her as "Theotokos" in the people's prayer showed this belief and reverence.[6]

Now this protrayal of Mary by Athanasius before 431 allows us to recognize two historical developments. On the one hand we can see how Athanasius influenced the future. His travels and acquaintances and authority made him a most important source of future expressions of faith and theology and prayer not only in what he said but in the way he explained what others could say in an orthodox manner. And that is what happened in the following years in the East and the West. Mary's titles of praise and the explanation of her role in the Gospel developed rapidly. On the other hand we can get a "glimpse" of what had been developing in the Church's memory of Mary before his time.

In Alexandria itself before the time of Athanasius the great teachers spoke about her. Origen lived in the first half of the third century. He was extremely influential as a teacher of Christian theology. He spoke of Jesus' purity and Mary's virginity as models for the people of his own day: Jesus for men, Mary for women. He spoke of Mary as a holy Jewess. She had to pursue holiness, for although she knew that Jesus was virginally conceived, she saw him die. Even though she was holy she needed to be redeemed. Only through the sword spoken of by Simeon was she able to "climb the mountain" of perfection. Her creatureliness, her holiness as a model for Christians, and her virginal motherhood were accepted ways of speaking about Mary at that time in Alexandria. We know that Theonas of Alexandria dedicated a church building to her memory in the late third century. So Origen's reverent words were not spoken in a vacuum.[7]

In the last years of the second century Clement of Alexandria, who taught in the famous catechetical school founded by his teacher Pantaenus, preceded Origen in recording reverence for Mary. He compared her virginal motherhood to that of the Church. He said that the Church's virginal motherhood was the more important of the two. This is interesting because of the ideas that were joined together. In the New Testament the Church is described as a chaste virgin, as the new Jerusalem, as our mother, and as a woman in labor. John's Gospel described the memory of Mary as mother and woman in the eschatological family or Church. Slowly a meditative process had been developing these images and joining them. The Church on earth and the Church in glory were compared to Mary as earthly mother of Jesus and as a mother who was in glory due to holiness as the gift of salvation from Jesus. Clement exemplifies this kind of meditative thinking in which Mary had a part.[8]

Was the same kind of memory of Mary going on in the communities beyond Alexandria? In the second century writings of Ignatius of Antioch (c. 110) and Justin Martyr (c. 160) we find statements that carry on the New Testament memory of Mary. They are creed-statements which imply professions of faith at baptismal or Eucharistic celebrations. The New Testament writings mention creeds that were statements made by believers in a liturgical context.[9] Since liturgy was just beginning the process of ritual formation that developed later, "liturgical context" has to be taken in the widest sense. Baptismal and Eucharistic contexts are probably the earliest ritual places where professions of faith occurred. These statements expressed faith that Jesus was the risen Lord and that he was human by his birth and death. (See Gal 4:4; 2 Tim 2:8; 1 Cor 15:5.) They imply a prayerful context of meditation on the Hebrew Scriptures in order to find words to express the meaning of Jesus and his work ("according to the Scriptures"). Out of these and other expressions in the New Testament writings, new combined statements were being made in the communities and are recorded by both Justin and Ignatius. Statements about faith that Jesus was born of a Jewish woman (Galatians) or of his Davidic descent (2 Timothy) are united to the infancy stories of Matthew and Luke. Jesus was "born of the virgin Mary." These new statements were professions of faith at a time when Jesus' humanity and divinity were being explained in new ways, some of which defended his humanity, and some of which were meant to console and support Christians during persecution (Ignatius). Some sought the explanations which would justify their beliefs to Jewish or Gentile scholars (Justin). The "virgin Mary" of whom Jesus was born was part of the eternal plan of God, the economy of salvation, wrote Ignatius. He cites Isaiah 7:14 to show how God planned her role. Justin looks backward to Eve as a prefigurement of Mary. Both were virgins, Eve in the old creation and Mary in the new creation.

The statements of Ignatius and Justin imply a context in which people are familiar with creedal statements, especially from the celebration of baptism and the Eucharist in their early Christian forms. These statements include the memory of Mary as Jesus' "virgin mother." And this memory of Mary was steeped in a reading of the Hebrew Scriptures and the New Testament to emphasize the unity of God's eternal plan, the "mystery" of Paul, in an ongoing economy of salvation. Because this salvation was given to Christians in the present, not just the past, people were consoled in persecution and found fuller understanding of their faith. They saw in Mary, as they saw in the martyrs and leaders of their communities, a person to be revered. She not only guaranteed the humanity of Jesus, but she was part of God's eternal plan, and it was her faith and joy and humility which reversed history (Justin). Her character was important even though details of her life were not emphasized.

For some Christians the details of Mary's life also became important. We humans are very curious about the personal details of the life of our models or revered characters. Reverence and curiosity about Mary led to apocryphal or fictional accounts of Mary's life. Birth and death, the themes which creeds and Gospels emphasized to show the meaning of Jesus, are used in these stories to fill in the biographical details which were not part of the message the canonical Gospels conveyed. The stories of the Hebrew Scriptures are used, not as meditations on the meaning of Jesus' salvation and Mary's role in it, the way Ignatius and Justin looked to Isaiah 7:14 or to Eve, but to describe imaginary scenes that would fill in details of Mary's life. They were reverent fabrications. The *Protogospel of James* is an example of this. It was probably composed by a Jewish Christian in the second century, perhaps in Alexandria. Some of the details, such as the name of Mary's parents, are still with us. Because of the strong reverence for Mary the stories lasted. Her holiness and virginity became "popularized."

The more theological approach of Ignatius and Justin continued, however. Irenaeus of Lyons (c. 200), who came from the eastern part of the Roman Empire, developed the parallel of Eve and Mary. He wrote that Mary's womb is the womb of salvation. He compared her obedience to God to the obedience of Jesus to the Father, and said that her obedience reversed creation and made her the "advocate of Eve." His usage of the word "advocate" implies a relationship between the memory of Mary and prayer life. It was not merely an academic interest that was present in the various Christian communities. Mary was part of the meditations and prayers of the people and their teachers. Irenaeus was a bishop who tried to unify Christians in various communities by his teachings. He must have thought that his teaching about Mary would have been acceptable to Christians despite persecutions and the problems they faced.

The memory of Mary in creedal statements, in meditations on the Hebrew Scriptures, in theological statements of explanation that were intended either to combat other explanations that divided communities or to comfort people facing difficulties, and in "apocryphal" stories was present and widespread before the time of Athanasius. Besides the writers we cited already there were the memories of Mary in the creedal statements of the *Apostolic Tradition*, attributed to Hippolytus of Rome (c. 215), in the paschal sermon of Bishop Melito of Sardis (c. 165), in the meditations on the Hebrew Scriptures done to find examples that could be applied to Mary in the *Apocryphal Ascension of Isaiah*, the *Odes of Solomon*, and the *Sybillene Oracles*. The catacombs of Priscilla were decorated with paintings of the adoration of the magi and of the mother and infant Jesus. There were monuments which marked her memory, such as the tomb of Abericius in Phrygia. There were pilgrimages in her memory made to Nazareth and Jerusalem. Mary's memory was kept alive in the Church in many ways and in many places before the time of Athanasius. She was revered as the virgin mother of the Lord with a role in the plan of God, a holy model of the kind of life Christians should lead, a human being glorified by her Son and remembered in the prayer life of Christians, who came from rich and poor environments in cities and villages.[10]

This is only a "glimpse" of what kind of memory of Mary was preserved between the time of the composition of the New Testament and the time when Athanasius could speak of a cultic "memory" and "role" of Mary in his Church community. Specialized studies can give more details of these early memories of Mary to those who wish to study them. Here it is enough to make the point that those writings which claim that 431 is the magic date when Marian devotion started and spread almost from nothing are not correct.

The New Testament memory of Mary's part in the story of Jesus was preserved and developed in the early Christian communities. As times changed and new problems came along, there were new applications of the New Testament memories. This occasioned development in the understanding of the faith of Christians. We know that it occurred in the great Trinitarian and Christological controversies and the statements of the ecumenical councils about how we should understand the New Testament when new problems made

Christians ask new questions. Development occurred in the meaning of the memory of Mary, too. The Church preserved the New Testament and presented the message of its traditional faith in ways that were both faithful to the past and meaningful to the present. In technical language we can say that the Church remembered, with the help of the Holy Spirit, with *hermeneutic*, to recapture the past, and with *anamnesis*, to present the reality of the past in each present moment.

As time went on this continued. The Church had to guide overenthusiastic statements into more moderate expressions, and to point out the need for more enthusiasm when memories became dim. The history of Marian devotion and doctrine is the story of how this happened. That long history is beyond our scope. However the part that liturgy played in this process from the start is something we will have to look at next.

REFERENCES

1. See Michael P. Carroll, *The Cult of the Virgin Mary* (Princeton: Princeton University Press, 1986). Carroll's knowledge of sources for understanding the New Testament, for historical data about Mary in the early Christian communities, and for the social makeup of the early Church is severely limited to the point of inexactitude in providing sufficient data for socio-psychological interpretation. (See pp. 4–5, 83–89, 103–106, 222.) His interpretation of the origin and development of the "cult," his interpretation of ritual and devotion, and his reliance on one school of psychological interpretation vitiate any conclusions he makes. The absence of current studies in the areas mentioned, e.g. Wayne Meeks in the demographic makeup of early Christianity or Victor Turner on ritual or any recognized exegete or historian of the Church since H. Graef, is glaring. On the ambiguous idea of worship of the "Mother Goddess," see J. Phillips, *Eve—The History of an Idea* (New York: Harper and Row, 1984), p. 176.

2. See R.M. Grant, *Augustus to Constantine* (New York: Harper and Row, 1970), pp. 10, 198ff, and *Early Christianity and Society* (New York: Harper and Row, 1977), pp. 35–36.

3. See H. Chadwick, *The Early Church* (New York: Penguin Books, 1977), p. 113, for the even earlier use of liturgy to defend orthodox doctrine by Origen. The idea that "the law of prayer establishes the law of belief" is much older than Prosper of Aquitaine (c. 455).

4. See Jaroslav Pelikan, *Development of Christian Doctrine— Some Historical Prologomena* (New Haven: Yale University Press, 1969), pp. 109ff, for the translation of Athanasius' words and commentary.

5. *Ibid.*, pp. 99–103.

6. *Ibid.*, pp. 114–119.

7. See E. Toniolo, O.S.M., "Padri della Chiesa," in *Nuovo Dizionario di Mariologia*, ed. by S. De Fiores and S. Meo (Milano: Edizioni Paoline, 1985), pp. 1053–1055. I found most of the summaries of Origen's ideas on Mary in English too one-sided. They examine Origen for answers to later questions.

8. *Ibid.*, p. 1053.

9. See C.F.D. Moule, *The Birth of the New Testament* (New York: Harper and Row, 1982), pp. 41ff. More emphasis on the liturgical context of New Testament confessions of faith is given by J.N.D. Kelly, *Early Christian Doctrines* (Cambridge University Press, 1967), pp. 62–65; Y. Congar, O.P., "Christ in the Economy of Salvation and in Our Dogmatic Tracts," in *Who Is Jesus of Nazareth?* (Concilium, Vol. 11) (New York: Paulist Press, 1966), p. 10; G. Wainwright, *Doxology—The Praise of God in Worship, Doctrine, and Life, cited before*, p. 48.

10. The best summary of data and ideas from various locations in the second century is an article by I. Calabuig, O.S.M., "Liturgia (origini)," in *Nuovo Dizionario di Mariologia* (*already cited*), pp. 768–787. It has no equal in English. On demography see W. Meeks, *The First Urban Christians* (Princeton: Princeton University Press, 1983), p. 199. English translations of some of the primary texts referred to can be found in H. Musurillo, *The Fathers of the Primitive Church* (New York: Mentor Omega Books, 1966).

6

RITUAL MEMORY— THE FOUNDATION OF MARIAN PIETY

The biggest problem that faced the Church as time went on and new groups of people were baptized was the preservation of unity. Unity was maintained in three vital areas. First of all there was the unity of belief and practice. Liturgy and the Gospels, creeds and theological explanations, morality and asceticism were not separated from each other. They were united in the "economy of salvation," the Christian way of life. Ascetical practices had to be founded on the Gospels and the liturgy. Theology had to be based on the creeds and cult of the community.

Second, the different linguistic and cultural communities or "local churches" which based their understanding of the mystery of salvation on the tradition they received from apostles or other disciples and leaders had to be united with other communities. Bishops of different communities met in councils together. Letters were written to other churches to exhort them to continue in the one faith and worship.

Third, the new developments which occurred in explanations of the creeds, in sacramental rituals, in hierarchical organization, and in devotional and ascetical practices had to be united in meaning with the old or traditional group memory in the "economy of salvation." The present had to be united with its foundation in the past.

Developments did occur. They did not emerge in a simple static growth, the way that 3 emerges from 2 in mathematics. A dynamic cultural process took place with the help of the Holy Spirit. There were ups and downs, struggles and controversies, love and bitterness in the process. Most of us are familiar with stories about the heated controversies that were involved in the development of the understanding of Jesus as God and man, or of the equality and distinction of the Persons in the Trinity. There were big problems in the development of the liturgy: the date of Easter, the catechumenate, the sacrament of reconciliation, admission of "apostates" to the sacraments. We saw how Athanasius struggled in the theological and liturgical controversies over the memory of Mary. In solving these problems the unity of the economy of salvation, the greater unity of the local churches in one Church, and the unity of new expressions with the traditional meaning of the faith was of crucial importance. It was also of importance in problems with which we are not so familiar. There was a problematic tendency, for example, to separate the unified elements of the economy of salvation from each other—liturgy from Gospels, theology from liturgy, and devotion from Scriptures and liturgy.

Not everything that happened in the process of development was good. Sometimes whole groups of Christians were lost to the unity of the Church because theology was separated from the practice of the Gospels. Bitterness and heat overcame love and light. And many tendencies of disruption continued throughout the centuries because of human weakness in the Church.

Because of this human weakness the Church is always in need of reform. In the process of reform the Church always goes back to the principle of threefold unity to resolve problems: the unity of the economy of salvation, unity among diverse communities, and unity of the present with the past. The Church always returns to its foundations in the Gospels and the liturgy.

This is precisely what the Second Vatican Council did in many areas of Church life that had become problems: theology and liturgy should be contemporary expressions of the early memories of the Church contained in the economy of salvation; diverse groups should symbolize in their own cultural ways the same faith as the universal Church; devotions and asceticism should be based on the gospels and the liturgy.

The renewal of Vatican II has accomplished many good things in theology and liturgy. The new Marian theology is returning to the

sources. The reform of the liturgical calendar and readings has provided us with a renewed memory of the Mary of the Gospels and the
early Church. Principles for new Marian devotional attitudes and
exercises have been spelled out. But not many such devotional exercises have been created. In this area of our life there is still some
disunity and silence.

The Second Vatican Council has told us that devotion to Mary
should be inspired by the liturgy and based on the Church's foundational memory of Mary. The liturgy is not all there is to prayer,
but it is the source and summit of all Christian prayer. Liturgical
memory brings us the Gospel.

Why the Church tells us these things is the topic of this chapter.
We will see that the Church said this because of *memory*. Whenever
new problems have emerged in the Church, the memory of the Church
which is "ritual memory" has been the key to development and to
unity. We will examine what this "ritual memory" means, and how it
applies to our contemporary devotion to Mary on a personal level.

Since we cannot have a living devotion in dead language nor
encounter Mary with the Lord in ways that are long gone, we will
need to consider also what might be contemporary ways to express
authentic devotion. Some brief suggestions may be of help.

Ritual Memory

Memory is the key to knowledge. That is true in all the various
ways we have knowledge: objective knowledge, personal knowledge, individual knowledge and group knowledge. We have to be
able to recognize, recall, recollect what we have come to *know about*
anything or anyone in order to say we really *know* it or them. If we
do not remember, we forget.

We enhance our knowledge of some *object* by study. To study
is to spend time in "cogitation," which means the collection of our
thoughts in analysis and synthesis in order to remember and understand.

To get to know a *person* better we spend time in relationship
with the other person. This is a behavioral process as well as an
intellectual one. Persons speak to each other by their actions and
words. Exterior manners portray interior life. The time spent together is a learning process in which recollection of what the other

person reveals about himself or herself can lead to mutual trust and understanding. As a relationship leads to deeper knowledge of the other person, that person becomes a part of my own personal memory. This is how we know and remember intimate friends, or relatives, or mere acquaintances.

What is true on an individual level is true for groups also. A tradition of learning in any group involves the preservation and communication of the wisdom of the past. Methods of study are handed on along with disciplinary fields of study in "schools" which enable new generations to *know about things* and to *know* them better through study. Groups remember *persons*, too. They hand on *knowledge* of *personal* characteristics of their heroes, founding figures, ancestors, and saints. They do this by organizing patterns of behavior in which symbolic words and gestures enable them to remember and to personally encounter these people in some way. These are *rituals*. They can be civic or religious.[1]

Examples of civic rituals are all around us. We pattern time into recurrent "holidays" at which time we do something symbolic in order to remember and to imitate the *personal* idealism of Columbus, the great persons of 1776, Abraham Lincoln, Dr. Martin Luther King, Jr., and others.

Religious rituals, which are a part of every human cultural group, are formally organized patterns of behavior and stories which use time and special places and gestures to remember the actions of *persons* in the past not only for imitation but for encountering them in the present. In every religion the divinity or archetypal sacred persons are encountered in rituals. Sacred stories explain how these persons reveal the meaning of life. Sacred actions of worship, prayer, and devotion enable the group to relate to divinity or sacred persons in the present. Knowledge of the past in its deepest sense includes personal relationship with the gods or ancestors in the present. Religious rituals re-present the persons who gave meaning to life in the past. At special times, for example the hunt, or the harvest, or the birth or death of someone, or the undertaking of a new home or a voyage, humans ritualized the meaning of the present by remembering in both word and deed the "primordial" time when the gods or ancestors gave meaning to the whole world or one aspect of it. They re-presented the foundation time and persons who established the meaning of life for the group. They expressed their religious belief and their unity as a people in these "rites." They recovered their *personal knowledge* and *relationship* with the sacred persons who continued to give meaning to their life.[2]

Such is the human way in which memory and knowledge are linked. Since the Church is human, it is the way of the Church also. In the mystery of the Church the human way reveals divine knowledge and presence. This is what we call "sacrament." The flesh of Jesus reveals his divinity. Human words and literary forms are inspired by God to reveal the divine message of salvation in the Scriptures. Human beings receive God's help to carry on the tradition of doctrine by which we come to *know about* God and Jesus. Human symbols and rituals are used to *encounter* God and Jesus and our saints in glory with God, to relate to them in our *personal* behavior.

The liturgical rituals of the Church were developed as ways in which the people of God could remember not only doctrines but the very persons involved in their sacred story. They are behavioral ways of knowing and encountering persons in order to remember them and to become involved with them. Their story and faith includes the promise of Christ to be present with his people and in his people always. Their rituals encounter Christ personally in his Church on earth and in heaven. They come together at sacred times and places to spend time bodily with the Lord and each other in the communion of saints, symbolizing the meaning of their life. They look backward to relate to God and his people in the present and to move forward. Thereby they will not forget how to live (see Jas 1:24–25; 1 Pet 3:15; 5:9).

Christian Ritual Memory

The earliest Christians were Jewish. They began to ritualize their memory of the Lord, since they were human, in Jewish ways, since they were Jews. They went to the temple rituals, prayed at the times sacred to the Jews, went to synagogue services for prayer and the reading of the Hebrew Scriptures. They remembered holy people of former days as models for behavior and as persons alive with God who still helped them (see Dt 32; Pss 155 and 134:1; Dan 3:86; Sir 44). But they were Christians, too. They had special practices and faith. The resurrection of the Lord colored all they read and heard in the Scriptures. They heard the story of Jesus' words and deeds "according to the Scriptures." They practiced "the breaking of bread," "the Lord's supper." They shared their goods with each other. They prayed "in vigil" as they awaited the fulfillment of the Lord's promises. They kept the day of the resurrection holy: Sunday. They "assembled" in a unity with each other and the Lord. They honored Christian heroes whose stories have come down to us in Gospels or who were martyred like Stephen. They used baptismal rituals of the Jews, but added their special profession of faith that "Jesus is Lord." They collected the words of Jesus. They pictured Jesus in "Hebrew" ways with the addition of newness: the new Moses, the new David, the fulfillment of all prophets.[3]

Christian rituals began to develop very early.[4] As more Gentiles became Christian their language, especially Greek, and symbols were incorporated into Christian worship of the Lord. Houses became the gathering place for the assembly. Hymns and psalms were composed. Jewish ritual laws were changed for Gentiles. After the temple of Jerusalem was destroyed a new understanding of temple and sacred place occurred (Jn 2:21; 4:21; Mt 12:6; Lk 2:46; 1 Cor 3:6; 6:19; Eph 2:21; Heb 9:11,24).

By the last third of the first century Christian liturgy was taking shape as a new and unique ritual memory and action. Rooted in the story of Jesus and the symbols of the Jews, it began to add new ways of expressing what Jesus meant to the new communities of people. In this context the Gospels were composed. The way they were composed tells us what kind of memory was important to the communities. The common structures of the Gospels exemplify *how* these people remembered. This helps us to understand the little we can discover about their actual ritual practices.

What was of primary importance for these late first century Christians was the proclamation ("kerygma") of the passion, death, and resurrection of Jesus. This was their primary belief and the central memory of their Eucharistic and baptismal rituals. They then moved backward to move forward, in the Jewish pattern of ritual memory. The Jews explained the meaning of each present moment by returning to the exodus and the great deeds of God. The Christians moved backward in the story of Jesus: his death and resurrection was explained by remembering his teachings ("didache") and deeds before he died. He was the Lord from the time of his conception. Then hymns were composed to describe his meaning as pre-existent and eternal Son and Lord. All of these moments of memory were recalled in order to understand the meaning of Jesus in the present.[5]

This movement backward helped the Christians to ritualize their memories. Baptismal and Eucharistic rituals developed new symbols and told Gospel stories of Jesus whose person was being encountered. We do not know much more than some details and the pattern of ritual memory of these early communities. Their cult had not yet become well organized. What we do know is that the stories of Jesus in the Gospels were preserved. They were proclaimed in word and in ritualized actions. We can also recognize that new symbolic expressions developed out of the original ones to keep the original *meaning* of these sacred memories of Jesus as new problems arose. This cultic tradition brought to new generations both *knowledge about* the personages in the Gospels and *personal knowledge* of them. It was at once doctrine and prayer.

Ritual and Devotion

This development of liturgical "memorial" included more than worship of the Holy Trinity. It included "devotion" to the heroic holy men and women remembered in the tradition. They were taken as *models* to be imitated and as *intercessors* at the throne of the Lord in heaven. Christians, like the Jews before them, did what all humans do in ritual. They remembered ancestors and heroes and heroines in their cult: Abraham, Moses, the apostles, the martyrs, and, in a special way, Mary (see Mk 14:3; Rev 3:12). Later they would remember confessors and virgins. All of these were sacramentally present with Christ, the same "yesterday, today, and forever" (Heb 13:7–8).

The memory of Mary was part of the Church's ritual life from the start. She had a "role" to play in the community's life, as Athanasius said. The Christian rituals handed on *knowledge about* Mary and her role in the work of Christ, and in a behavioral way the people came *to know* her. They remembered her *meaning* in the past and in the present. They proclaimed her role in the Gospels and in creeds within their baptismal and Eucharistic rituals—the creed that Jesus was "born of a woman," "of Davidic descent," became "born of the Virgin Mary," which brought to mind her title and name and meaning in the Gospels, a Christological and ecclesiological meaning.

It was the Gospel memory of Mary which the Church made present in each age in its rituals. The Gospel *meaning* of Mary was expressed in symbols and ways of understanding which belonged to the people, in their own time and culture, and with their own problems. This meaning of Mary was always a part of the meaning of Christ for the Church. Through these symbolic ritual actions the Church remembered where the group came from, who it was, and where it was going. Mary meant someone special to the group, as it saw itself. She had had a special role in the life and memory of the Church from its origins.

The original memory of Mary in the Gospels was a foundational memory for the Church. This was the memory that had to be preserved and presented again as time went on. It was the foundation for knowing Mary and for knowing her role in the faith life of each Christian.

We saw what that original memory was. The Church remembered her first of all as a holy Jewish woman. God "did great things for her" because he "regarded" her as a holy person who heard his word and kept it. That is the way in which she became the mother of the Lord. It was not her blood maternity of Jesus, taken out of this context of her holiness, which made her memorable. It was her maternity as a woman chosen to be mother because of her characteristics as one of the "faithful remnant," "the poor of God," ready to be his "servant." Given the cultic context in which the Gospels were composed—a time when the Christian communities were developing their ritual memories—we can see *why* and *how* this memory of Mary became the foundation for devotion to her.

At this time when the Church began to develop its normative doctrines and rituals and devotions Mary was remembered as a *model*. The profession of faith that Jesus was "born of the Virgin Mary" carried on the memory that Jesus was born of a model woman. The "virgin" was the "virgin of the Gospels." "Virgin" was a title that summed up all the Gospel memories of Mary. In the fashion of symbols and rituals she is remembered and presented again in such a way that her meaning as "virgin" is explained by the words and deeds that make up the behavior of the ritual, especially the Gospel stories and actions associated with baptism and the Eucharist. She is remembered formally, distant from everyday details such as you would find in a contemporary biography. The ritual distance or formality allows for people to apply the archetype or model to their own personal lives—lives that differed from individual to individual. She is remembered and presented as a *universal model*, an archetypal focal point, for "all generations" to identify with. As a special model for Christians in their memory and encounter with Christ, the memory of her became the foundation for a devotion to her. No one can miss the significance of this memory of Mary in a Church becoming more and more Gentile. Mary is the humble Jewish woman who served God and was rewarded with God's loving mercy and with the Holy Spirit, so that she gave birth to the Lord. She was a global model for all who sought God's loving mercy and the incarnation of Christ in their life through the Holy Spirit. That is *why* the ritual memory of Mary became the source of devotion to her.

How she was remembered by the Church, and re-presented in the rituals, makes it even clearer how the liturgy became the source of devotion to her. In the Gospels and in the rituals which depended on or used the Gospels, Mary was remembered and symbolized as more that just a model. She is not remembered only for purposes of imitation. The Church remembered that she would be "called" holy by each generation (Lk 1:48). She is to be *devoutly* remembered. She is portrayed as having a special role to play in the Christian communities' sacred memory of Jesus. She will have a *cultic memory* and *role* in Christian life, as Athanasius summed it up.

Mary's imitability and special role are structured into the Gospel narratives. Luke and John bring out elements of how she is the model for Christians who must take up the cross as Jesus did (see Col 1:24; Rom 6:5; Mk 8:34–35; 9:30,39,44; 13:13,23,30; Heb 12:22–24; Rev 6:9–10). For Luke, Mary is the woman whose heart was to be pierced by the "sword of discernment." She heard the word of God and kept that word. Therefore she will be called "blessed" by "all generations." She did not understand the meaning of Jesus' words and deeds, yet pondered them in her heart and persevered through the cross and resurrection to the time of the gift of the Spirit in the Acts of the Apostles. She tells all hearers of the word that God lifts up the lowly and inverses worldly values.

John's Gospel remembers these characteristics of Mary in its own way. She perseveres to the "hour" of the cross and glorification of Jesus. It is her love which, as a gift of God, enables her to persevere, just as love enabled the "beloved disciple" to participate in the cross and glorification of the Lord. John presents her as the mother of Jesus and the "woman" of the new creation of God's love who is the exemplar of love which participates in the cross.

John and Luke bring out the specialness of Mary's exemplarity by portrayals of her relationship to the Holy Spirit. In John's Cana sign it is Mary who notices (in the ever-present tense of the reading of the story) that the people in messianic times, at the wedding feast, need the wine of the Spirit. Only she and the "servants" of the banquet know where the wine can come from. John tells us that the Spirit comes from Jesus' cross and glorification. And at that "hour" it is to his mother and to the beloved disciple that the Spirit is handed over in a special way. Through the gift of the Spirit Jesus makes his disciples to be not only servants but loving friends and children of God, his brothers and sisters in the new family of the Father. The Spirit will enable them to say "yes" to his commandment of love, just as he says "yes" to the Father's will. The Spirit will enable them to love with the very love of God and live with the very life of God. The beloved disciple exemplifies this new life in the Spirit. And Mary is given to him as his new "mother." That is how her special exemplarity is developed in John: she is given to Christians as their example and as their mother when they receive the Spirit and become loving disciples. And like the beloved disciple they must take her into their lives in that role.

Luke remembers the relationship of Mary to the Spirit, too. Mary said "yes" to the Father, just as Jesus did. (See Mk 7:28; Mt 5:37; Lk 12:8; 14:27; 20:7; 21:13,19; 22:42; Jn 21:16; 2 Cor 1:19–20.) This was her obedience and service of God. Because of these characteristics God loved her and she was "overshadowed" by the Holy Spirit. Her attitude of obedient service exemplified how Christians should imitate Christ, God's obedient servant (Phil 2:1–11; Gal 5:25). However Luke remembers her as more than this. She brings the gifts of life in the Spirit to both Elizabeth and the unborn John the Baptist. Elizabeth gives her special veneration because of that: "Who am I that the mother of my Lord should come to me?" So Luke remembers her maternity as a gift to all who live in the

Spirit. She brings the Spirit's gifts to all disciples: wonder and faith and joy. How important that this sacred memory be part of baptismal and Eucharistic ritual invocations of the Holy Spirit.

This formal memory of Mary in the Gospels has a richness that goes beyond the memory of her as an example of Christian life. She is not remembered for biographical details in the way that Paul or Zacchaeus or Stephen is. She is more formal and distant. She is remembered more for her theological meaning, more like an archetypal model in the way Abraham and Moses (2 Pet 2:10) and the great men and women of Israel's past are remembered. The Gospels insist that she is not remembered as part of the natural family of Jesus, his blood mother only. That is the way pagan goddesses, mothers of divine and semi-divine children, were remembered. She is an archetypal figure for all times (Lk 1:48). But she is remembered in this way because she had a role in the Gospel of Jesus, just as others were remembered for that reason (Mt 26:13).

Mary's role in the ritual memory of Jesus was that she who was a holy woman and virgin mother of Jesus was also a special gift from the Lord to every Christian. She is given to disciples as "mother" in the new family of God, the new creation. As "mother," like the "woman" Eve, who was remembered as "mother of all the living," she brings the gifts of the Spirit to the new sons and daughters of God. She is human, but very special in holiness and in her role in what Jesus brought about. She is for all people, so that while her role is intimate, it is described formally in terms of all the holy models of Jewish history.

These original symbols by which the group of the faithful formally remembered Mary's role in salvation were powerful ones. It cannot be surprising to anyone that very soon after the time of origins there was a development, as we saw in Chapter Five. New symbols and devotions carried on the original meaning and memory of Mary. We do not need fanciful rationalizations about the influence of paganism to explain why she was soon revered under the title "Theotokos." The original group memories of the faithful—memories that were doctrinal and liturgical and devotional at once—had to be expressed in the language and situations that were developing in new communities of Christian people with new problems. Soon after the early centuries she would, quite naturally in the way of cultural development, be portrayed in imperial robes as mother of the "Pantokrator" and "seat of wisdom" by Byzantine Christians. She would come to be called "queen" and "universal queen" and "tender mother" and by other titles in times of royalty and emphasis on the tenderness of women. The original symbols were preserved by the Church in its memory and presented anew in each age.

It is also true that we should not be surprised that at times the original symbols of the Church were corrupted. The Church is human in its membership, not only divine by the gift of grace. It is not the kingdom of God in its final perfection. It is a net containing good fish and bad fish. It is made up of rich and poor, strong and weak, learned and unlearned, sinners and saints. That is who we are, what we are like. Therefore it should not be surprising that Mary was called a goddess by semi-pagan *literati* in the High Renaissance, and painted like one at the same time. Nor should we pretend utter astonishment that preachers waxed eloquent in praising her, even at the expense of God and the truth of Christ's lordship and mercy. We cannot honestly feign surprise that poor and uneducated Christians think of her as God's "mama," and never think of God. And it is understandable that an accretion of symbols in liturgy and devotion covered over the original Gospel symbols until they were forgotten. It was because they, like any group, were human in their ways, religious and civic, that Christians would constantly need reform to overcome poor symbolism that developed in cult, and poor theology about Mary that developed in the age of reason. The Church always has needed reform and always will need it.[6]

Precisely here we should feel the cutting challenge of our times. The Second Vatican Council and Pope Paul VI have clearly pointed out to us the need and direction for change that is experienced in the Church today: we must recover the Gospel symbols of Mary and the Church's traditional memory of her, and we must present what that memory means in the best contemporary ways that we can find.

Return to the Foundations of Devotion

The Second Vatican Council addressed our need for change in the Church. Our doctines and liturgy and practices of devotion had arrived at a point by the 1960's where abstract reasoning about myriads of propositions in theology and where formal rituals were expressed in the language and symbols of bygone days and a multiplicity of devotions were practiced as if they were more important than the sacraments. In order for people to understand their faith as it was handed on by the Church and to participate in the rituals which were their very own group memories and encounters with God and to have devotional practices consonant with the Gospel, there had to be a "renewal." The Gospel memories of the Lord had to be made new and present again. This was true in doctrine, in liturgy and in devotions.[7]

The Church issued formal guidelines for this renewal. Theologians were to take care that doctrine be based on the best study of the Sacred Scriptures. The mystery of Christ and the Church must be central in doctine if it is to express the belief of the Church. Theology should keep the experience of the communities of the Church in mind in order to have a pastoral benefit for the Church. And so the renewal of theology and docrine began.

The Church has undertaken a renewal of all liturgical rituals, giving this work a primacy of importance. The liturgy is the "source" and "summit" of Christian life. Liturgical rites have to express the sacred memory of the Gospels and the development of that memory in Church tradition in order to present the mystery of Christ among today's people. People have to be able to participate in the rituals in order to encounter Christ the Lord, to know him personally. The same is true of Mary and the saints in the liturgy. Since the promulgation of the *Constitution on the Sacred Liturgy* in 1963 which began the work of adapting structures, language, and gestures to the Gospel past and to the present, many other instructions have been issued as new symbols were approved for liturgical expression over the following years. Local groups in dioceses of every ethnic culture had to come up with contemporary symbolic expressions which had to be approved by appropriate authorities is Rome.

All of this took a lot of effort and time. Guidelines were set up for the renewal of devotional practices, too. Devotions that were not founded on the Gospel reverence for the mother of the Lord and the Church's authentic tradition of reverence for the saints had to cease. What was merely sentimental or what was an exaggeration had to cease. New ways of devotion that flowed from the liturgical encounter with the Lord had to be expressed. These had to come from and speak to the hearts of contemporary men and women. Not too much time was spent on this renewal. Many devotions just ceased. That was not surprising in a way, since theology and the liturgy had to be renewed before their effect could be felt in ways of expressing devotion. By 1974 theology and liturgy had been renewed adequately enough to get down to this challenge.[8]

In 1974 Pope Paul VI issued the Apostolic Exhortation *Marialis Cultus* to spur on the challenge of renewal of Marian cultic expression and devotion. He wanted to ensure that Church renewal would continue in the area of devotional life. The renewal that had already been undertaken in doctrine and the liturgy were the guidelines he used to encourage new ways of devotion to Mary. The worship of the community in liturgical rituals indicated the kind of devotion to be given to Mary, and to other holy people since she is regarded as the model among the saints. Divine worship belongs to God, the Holy Trinity, alone. The reverence of veneration is given to Mary and the saints in the formal public acts of the worship of God. The way in which Mary and the saints are venerated in the liturgy show us the way we can have devotional attitudes and actions toward them outside the liturgy.

Pope Paul noted first of all that the renewal that had already occurred pointed out to us that our contemporary way of remembering the special relationship we have with Mary must be based on the way Mary is remembered in the Gospels. Mary must be remembered and venerated for the role she played in the story of Jesus. All expressions of reverence for her today must therefore be Christological and ecclesiological. She must be remembered as the model of response to the Father, the Son, and the Holy Spirit. She is a model of the Church remembered by the Church: model and mother. That is the way the renewed liturgy remembers her in the revised sacred texts and sacred calendar of feasts.

The Kind of Devotion Which the Church Asks of Us

The Pope went on to challenge the Church to find ways to express this veneration outside the liturgy. He said that in order to express the *meaning* of Mary as a model and mother in daily life we have to use the expressions distinctive to our own culture. This de-

mands both creativity and evaluation. Therefore he supplied criteria we can use to evaluate the form and content of contemporary
expressions of the traditional meaning of Mary. They must be based
on contemporary understanding of the Gospels. They must carry on
the renewed liturgical ways of expressing her memory. Also, they
have to be ecumenically sensitive. That is, they should take care to
express the Gospel and not the kind of exaggerated expressions, of-
fensive to our Protestant and Jewish brothers and sisters, which
have at times been used in the past. They should also show deep
awareness and respect of the memory of Mary preserved and handed
on in the Eastern Churches. Finally, our expressions of devotion
have to be in consonance with the psycho-sociological world of today, which we can become more aware of through various academic
studies outside of the area of theology.[9]

Now this was a challenge given to the Church—to all of us—
in an official statement of the Pope—an Apostolic Exhortation, not
just an address. With those critieria which he spelled out as guidelines, we have to find new ways to express the memory of Mary in
our devotional life. This is a challenge to inventiveness and creativity, not to a theology but to what Amos Wilder so well described
as a "theopoetic." It covers all the affective ways we express meaning as we remember Mary: music, art, writing, reading, speaking,
our psychological and social needs, clarity, beauty.

To meet this challenge the first thing that we have to do is to
discover *themes*. These will focus on our cultural problems and ac-
complishments. They will clarify the "signs of the times," the
places in our life and in our world that demand the presence of
Christ. They will have to be discovered through reading and experience, through discussion and criticism in groups. Only after
themes have been discovered and clarified can they be shaped and
structured into "exercises" which lead us to prayer and action. To
shape such structures there will have to be a search for the language
and music and kinds of action which express well in our day the
Church's tradition of Mary's meaning, especially the Gospels. This
will demand experimentation, discussion, evaluation, and revision.

After the discovery of themes, then, there will still be a lot of
work for individuals with particular talents, and for groups. The
Pope has asked us to undertake a difficult task. But only if we do
so will there be a good new devotional life to take the place of the

old which we miss so much. If people did that work in the past—and they did it and should be given credit—we can do it, too. Then we will have the exercises that will keep our devout memory alive during our day, and in our generation we call Mary "blessed."[10]

What kind of *themes* might be suggested as a possible aid to help all of us, in general, to meet our challenge? There are several glaring signs of the times. It is up to each of us to read them for ourselves and to express their significance for our faith. Once we have undertaken to do this for ourselves we will be ready to discuss them in groups. I would like to suggest several themes and how a serious group of Christians might shape and pattern them in symbolic gestures, to spur you on to do your part as a rememberer of what God has done for us.

One of the most insistent realizations about our times, which keeps coming to us between the lines of so many issues and problems that we are made aware of, is *globalization*.[11] Every human group is in several ways dependent upon all the rest of the humans in the world. The issues of today remind us that most of the daily facts of life involve *world* economics, politics, standards of living and values. The memory of Mary in the Gospel has much to say about how this fact of *globalization* or *world interdependence* relates to our faith. Mary is the universal model of a human being who affirms the word and work of God. She is the woman of the great "yes." In her day and age she found meaning in the world through her faith—and the meaning she found reverberated on the whole human race. This lady, our holy sister Mary, listened to and pondered, despite her problems, the revelation of God. And God regarded her search for meaning. He filled her with love and justice and joy and peace. And she carried these gifts to others. She was good and spread goodness. She is a model for men and women all over the world, from India to Peru, no matter what their religion. Many Moslems already see her in this role. It would be easy to shape this theme for meditation through such actions as inviting a person from another culture or religion to a time of prayer on this theme. Readings from creation stories, such as Genesis 1, or even those of other religions, say Bantu, could be used for Christian reflection. Art about children from around the world, even if it is on posters or slides, could be used as visual symbols of the universal human being. Contemporary Marian art could be used. If Bill Hawk's "Annunciation," or some equivalent piece of art, were on show at a local museum, as it was in St. Louis, Missouri not long ago, the group could journey to see it as part of the group action. Prayers from the week of Church Unity liturgies could be used. The point would be the expression of how God our Father moves all of us to hear his word in creation, and how Jesus the Lord moves us to do the same with all our brothers and sisters on earth.

Another theme of our day is the *dignity of woman*. This holy woman Mary was strong. She did not hesitate to ask "How is this possible?" when confronted with God's own revelation. She pondered the meaning of God's words and works in her heart. She was free and independent, an amazing model coming from her historical social situation. She sought what was good and acted on what she found. In the process she was open to God in his most mysterious ways, and she was open to the people who whould seek the will of God, like Elizabeth and John the unborn Baptist. She was married, but she was a virgin, a model of seriousness for married and for single women. She was strong in her love. She spoke out. Through her freedom the new creation of Jesus came about, in which there is neither male nor female. She is the mother of a new family of God, a new world order of Christian love. She was not "out of reach," a fanatic, someone given to esoteric miracles: she knew poverty, the life of a Jewish village, and the wonders of God that are always close at hand. She became the model for all persons of faith, showing the evil of human egoism due to distinctions of strong and weak or rich and poor in social life. This theme could use the Magnificat of Luke's Gospel for meditation and singing, and pictures of women and men from around the world who are equally "images of God" and called to be brothers and sisters in one family of the Father. A poem could be read. A story of the "despairing women" of tragic politically unjust situations in Latin America could be read. A commentary on how societies often presume the inferiority of women to men could be made. A prayer for peace and equality with a reading from Galatians on the equality of male and female, Greek and Jew, and all whom society can discriminate against, could be read, with that creed from Galatians being a prayer stimulus: Jesus was "born of a woman, born under the law."[12]

Poverty is a theme of the words of Mary's Magnificat, too. The song of Mary has reverberations that go far back into the history of

God's special people, the Jews. The physically poor, the socially poor, the downcast and trodden, and all those deprived of any riches, even psychological and spiritual riches, are people special to God in many ways. We are all poor before the divinity: we wear the ashes of Adam on Ash Wednesday. We are only mortals. We could read of how the Lord Jesus emptied himself in Philippians 2. We could tell about sharing our gifts with our brothers and sisters, especially the least ones. We could meditate on the shepherds who found the mother and child together. There are many things we could do to shape a devotion to Mary, woman of the poor. She can model the attitudes we need and pray for us to attain them with the help of God. She exemplifies the justice of God as the motive we need.[13]

Besides globalization, poverty, and the dignity of woman which are themes pressing upon every human today in our quest for freedom and dignity, there are many other themes which can be shaped into expressions of affection and devotion as we follow Christ with Mary as our model. *The crisis of values in our life* is another one, for example. Here we can focus on the assumption or glorification of Mary, the holy woman and virgin mother of the Lord.[14] *Eros* and *thanatos* are two prongs of the horns which often gore each of us to pain and anxiety today. Our passions, whether for flesh pleasures or for material satisfactions, must be controlled and shaped into love for God and his children, our brothers and sisters all over the world, beginning at home. Death and all the little deaths of our time on earth, ranging from divorce and separation from loved ones to relationships gone bad and from addiction to chemicals to greed for superficial material appearances, can become a cross without Christ, a "tale told by an idiot, full of sound and fury and signifying nothing." The Christian man and woman are not exempt from the world in which all live. Rich and poor in every nation are subject to the great illusions of life in time. Yet all thirst for the perfection and utter goodness which belongs only to God in eternity. The quest for meaning is always a quest for unity with God our final goal deep down in our psyches and hearts. Mary exemplifies how the Christian man and woman must shape their life during the quest for meaning and fulfillment. She is a woman who says *yes* to Love in the way she shapes her sexual life—virginity—because she knows what she is doing, and she is doing it in openness and response to God. She is the kind of person who listens to the word of God, ponders it in her heart, and keeps it despite difficulties. She recognizes the call of God—that movement of the Spirit which all humans can recognize, be they Christian or non-Christian, in the things of creation, the things that happen in life, which are the call of being (Heidegger) or the voice of God. So she shapes her erotic life. And she perseveres through the cross to the resurrection, through difficulties to meaning—and not only to delayed gratification. She sows and reaps, but goes deeper into her human soil than superficial gratifications. And she receives the Spirit—for John at the cross, and for Luke in the primitive new family of God. Then, like the martyrs who won the crown of glory, who ran the race and received the prize—two early New Testament figures of speech for life with God in heaven—she went with Christ, her Son, to her Father and God. She attained meaning and happiness. This is something all can relate to today. We can express to God our faith that he will help us to do what she did, and we can work at hearing the word of God each day. This could be a morning prayer. It could be put into the shape of remembering the new creation as we begin each day—perhaps with Cat Stevens' rendition of the old Gaelic song "Morning Has Broken," which reminds us of the creation.

There are so many issues. Some are new and pressing. Some press us to joy and sadness and have been with us always. If we thematize them, relate them to Mary as our model and our glorified mother, use contemporary language and music and art, we can as groups remember the story of the Lord and carry the power of the liturgy into the thick and thin of daily life. We can update the old, create new patterns, evaluate what we do. We can. In fact we have to, or we will forget who we are.

It is so easy to say that "we have to do this or that." Nothing will happen if we do not feel that "we have to" do something. We need motivation. One positive way to attain the needed motivation is to read and to study. Each of us should use our God-given intelligence to guide our prayers and daily life as Christians. If we don't, we will suffer for it. We will never appreciate the Church and the Church's basic meaning: to give us a memory of who we are. We won't know who we are. We will have vague intimations of the Gospels and of the Church that is more than the newsworthy Vatican. We will be persons in search of an identity. Even sadder, we will not even know that that is what we are. If we study good theological writings that challenge our minds and feed our deepest hungers, we will start to know who we are. This will make us once more people of the Gospel—people who love their liturgy. People motivated in this way will reverence the memory of Mary.

There is a negative spur to motivation today, too. We see increasing numbers of people turning to apocalyptic ideas in religion and to alleged visions and miraculous phenomena. In many cases this demonstrates a thirst for God which is not being met in the teaching and liturgy of the Church. Such people treasure a memory of Mary that is not based on the Gospel so much as it is on their psychological needs or on "personal revelations" that are far from what the meaning of the Gospels reveals. This will eventually cause hurt in many quarters. The only remedy is to guide our emotions and images by the Church's teaching and tradition, the Scriptures and the liturgy. To have these as our guide we will have to have the renewal that the Second Vatican Council began. There must be good preaching, good liturgy, good writing, and availability of Scripture study for each person and group in every community.

The onus of seeing that such things actually happen falls on each one of us. Pope Paul VI started the encouragement. Each of us must see that we are self-renewed and encourage others to get involved. Women's participation is essential. They can begin to phrase for us, both men and women, in our local communities, what being a woman means and how this relates to Mary and to each of us. Only if that happens will we be able to understand the meaning of Mary and of Mary's relationship to the Church in our own time. Fundamentally Mary is "the holy woman." In our day the meaning of that has been covered over by centuries of male-centered symbols and meanings. How can a man say what it is to be a woman? How dare a man say "women are this or that"? For too long the Church has had a male-centered understanding of Mary as "the successsful woman," "the powerful woman," the "woman who meets our needs." Rarely have we seen the image of Mary as the independent woman, the strong woman, the leader.

New issues are here to stay: the feminine attributes of God, the leadership role of women in ministry, sexist language, the effect of the monopoly of maleness in our understanding of our tradition. If we put off the integration of honest study of these issues into our theology and liturgy, it will be too late to surmount the growing gap between the people who are not scholars and the scholars who study these issues. This will affect all devotions from the viewpoint of what Pope Paul VI called "the psycho-sociological field in which man lives and works." The Pope says that "what is needed is effort."[15]

An example of the effect of renewal in Irian Jaya can show us the good that can come from our effort. People without a way to gain justice began to demand changes in the way they were paid and treated by foreign economic developers. They did this because of the liturgy. "They confronted the storekeeper for doubling prices on some items . . . helped the uneducated workers count their change and demanded redress on cheated transactions." They said that they did this because "in our liturgies we learn that Christ is present among us, in our sago groves, in our traditions, in one another. Christ is there but it is up to us if he stays."[16]

We could say that "in our liturgies we learn that Mary is present among us as our mother and model. She is present with us as our helping sister in our homes, our streets, our schools, our places of work and recreation. She is there with Christ. But it is up to us if she stays." It is along the lines of what St. Augustine once said to God as he searched for him in his memory: "You were with me, but I was not with you." It is up to us to be with Mary so that she stays with us.

Elie Wiesel once said that "the opposite of history is not myth, it is forgetfulness." If we forget our history, we will not be anything in the present. If we are not anyone or anything, we will be silent about our history, amnesiac. But if we turn to the Gospels we will live our historical identity once more. We will celebrate it in our liturgy. Mary will be our model. We will have devotion to her in a balanced way. We will not be silent.

Mary noticed that the people at the banquet had no wine. She knew how to get it. She got it for them. The ones who were "servants" knew where she got it. If we become servants of God, we too will know. We will actually remember to do what Mary said: "whatever he tells us." But to be faithful servants we are going to have to remember, to pray "May we who honor the memory of the Virgin Mary come one day to your banquet of eternal life."[17]

REFERENCES

1. See V.W. Turner, *The Ritual Process: Structure and Anti-Structure* (Chicago: Aldine Press, 1969); G.S. Worgul, *From Magic to Metaphor—A Validation of the Christian Sacraments* (New York: Paulist Press, 1980), pp. 49–110; L.L. Mitchell, *The Meaning of Ritual* (New York: Paulist Press, 1977).

2. See M. Eliade, *Australian Religions* (Ithaca: Cornell University Press, 1973), pp. 40ff, 82ff, and *A History of Religious Ideas, Vol. 2* (University of Chicago Press, 1982), pp. 338, 410.

3. See M. McNamara, M.S.C., "The Liturgical Assemblies and Religious Worship of the Early Christians," in *The Crisis of Liturgical Reform*, Concilium 42 (New York: Paulist Press, 1969), pp. 20–36; J. Lecuyer, C.S.Sp., "The Liturgical Assembly: Biblical and Patristic Foundations," in *The Church Worships*, Concilium 12 (New York: Paulist Press, 1966), pp. 3–18; R. Taft, S.J., *The Liturgy of the Hours in East and West* (Collegeville: Liturgical Press, 1986), pp. 3–12.

4. See A. Kavanagh, *The Shape of Baptism: The Rite of Christian Initiation* (New York: Pueblo Publishing Co., 1978), pp. 20–25; R.H. Fuller, "Christian Initiation in the New Testament," in *Made, Not Born* (University of Notre Dame Press, 1976), pp. 7–31; L. Ligier, S.J., "The Biblical Symbolism of Baptism in the Fathers of the Church and the Liturgy," in *Adult Baptism and the Catechumenate*, Concilium 22 (New York: Paulist Press, 1967), pp. 16–30; J.A. Jungmann, S.J., *The Mass*, edited by M. Evans and translated by J. Fernandez (Collegeville: Liturgical Press, 1976), pp. 5–33.

5. See J.A. Fitzmyer, S.J., *A Christological Catechism* (New York: Paulist Press, 1982), pp. 41, 69; H. Neil Richardson, "The Old Testament Background of Jesus as Begotten of God," *Bible Review*, 2/3, Fall 1986, pp. 22–27.

6. D. Flanagan, *The Theology of Mary* (Hales Corners: Clergy Book Service, 1976), p. 85, gives an example of exaggerated piety. A. Dulles, S.J. explains rationalism in theology in *The*

Survival of Dogma (New York: Image Books, 1973), pp. 120, 205. Vatican II's *Constitution on the Sacred Liturgy*, No. 62, points out the corruption of symbols.

7. Examples of the call to renewal can be found in Vatican II's Decrees on *The Training of Priests*, Nos. 13–22, and on *Ecumenism*, Nos. 70–76, and in the *Constitution of the Sacred Liturgy*, Nos. 14–43. See W. Kern, *New Liturgy and Old Devotions* (New York: Alba House, 1979), pp. 15, 38.

8. For a description of the present situation and ongoing renewal in liturgy and doctrine, see K.W. Irwin, "The Constitution on the Sacred Liturgy," in *Vatican II and Its Documents—An American Reappraisal*, edited by T.E. O'Connell (Wilmington: M. Glazier, Inc., 1986), pp. 9–38.

9. See *Marialis Cultus*, Nos. 2–15 and 29–39 in Paul VI, *Mary— God's Mother and Ours* (Boston: St. Paul Editions, 1979), pp. 100–113 and 128–140.

10. The need for symbolic creativity is felt in every religious group today. The challenge is well expressed by Amos N. Wilder, *Theopoetic—Theology and the Religious Imagination* (Philadelphia: Fortress Press, 1976). See W. Brennan, O.S.M., "Theology and Poetry," *Catholic Library World*, 52 (1980), pp. 198ff.

11. For a succinct and moving summary of this issue, see "Abdus Salam" by R.M. Kidder, *The Christian Science Monitor*, December 9, 1986, pp. 28–29.

12. For background reading which would aid in shaping this theme, see Sharon D. Welch, *Communities of Resistance and Solidarity—A Feminist Theology of Liberation* (New York: Orbis Books, 1985); Joan C. Engelsman, *The Feminine Dimension of the Divine* (Philadelphia: Westminster Press, 1979), pp. 121–156; Rosemary R. Ruether, *Mary—The Feminine Face of the Church* (Philadelphia: Westminster Press, 1977).

13. This theme could link up the Magnificat and the dogma of the immaculate conception, too. For theological reflection as background to do this I would suggest J.B. Metz, *Faith in His-*

tory and Society (New York: Seabury Press, 1980), pp. 110–114 and 200–204 ("Dogma Is Dangerous Memory").

14. Helpful reading for this theme would be D. Flanagan, "Eschatology and the Assumption," *The Problem of Eschatology*, Concilium 41 (New York: Paulist Press, 1969), pp. 135–146, and Gina Hens-Piazza, "Woman: Symbolic Priority of the Church as Kingdom–Liberation Mariology," *Marianum* 47 (1985), pp. 216–224.

15. *Marialis Cultus*, Nos. 31, 34. Pope Paul VI underlined the importance of *effort* to relate the two areas of biblical-liturgical memory of Mary and ecumenical-anthropological presentation of that memory today. He said that certain attitudes of piety would be contrary to these "directives," especially an "exaggerated search for novelties or extraordinary phenomena" (No. 38). Today the emphasis on visions seems to fall in line with the kind of piety which the Pope said is contrary to the mind of the Church. More people seem to flock to scenes of strange phenomena than to the liturgies or to the reading of the Scriptures in order to understand Mary. It is the duty of pastors and all Church leaders to cultivate the directives which correct such "piety." It will take a great deal of effort to encourage up-to-date reading required to do this. Church leaders should be familiar with works on Mary's place in Scripture and theology. It will not be enough to merely "wait" to see what happens in popular movements concerned with visions, moving statues, and crying ikons. They should make the effort to read such works as Karl Rahner's "Mary and the Christian Image of Woman," in his *Faith and Ministry—Theological Investigations XIX*, translated by E. Quinn (New York: Crossroad, 1983), pp. 211–217, and R.E. Brown's article "More Polemical than Instructive: R. Laurentin on the Infancy Narratives," *Marianum* 47 (1985), pp. 188–207.

16. Quoted by Frank Maurovich in "Indonesia's Hidden Jewel," *Maryknoll* 80/5, May 1986, p. 15.

17. Liturgy of the Common of the Blessed Virgin Mary, 3. Prayer After Communion.